Hoovering
the Roof

The first anthology from
the East Dulwich Writers' Group

London, UK

ISBN 978-0-9564218-0-7

Cover and Illustrations by RHKW
Printed by – lightning source.

This book is dedicated to the friends and families of all the contributors, for putting up with our obsession.

EDWG would like to acknowledge the support of the Bookseller Crow on the Hill in Crystal Palace and all the other independent bookshops who enrich our reading lives. Thanks also Jack's Cafe in East Dulwich - the home of the EDWG coffee caucus.

Introduction

Once upon a time, way back at the fag end of the last millennium, a lone writer decided he'd like to meet up with other local authors to share their words. He put cards in shop windows (this was long before the days of internet forums) and half a dozen people responded. The East Dulwich Writers' Group was formed.

To begin with, the group met in the back room of a local café. After the first few meetings, they decided it would be more comfortable to meet in each other's homes, where they would have access to kettles, toilets, back gardens and – yes – roofs.

Twelve years later, over a hundred people have joined the mailing list for the group. In spite of the huge numbers, EDWG has remained intimate and informal, retaining an ethos of mutual support and constructive criticism. The ages of our members range from teens to octogenarians and we reflect the diversity of culture and class in this corner of South East London.

We have people at every stage of their writing career, from absolute beginners to published authors and competition winners. All those who have attended regular meetings have appreciated the feedback and advice, as well as the motivation provided by the group. For some of us, EDWG has literally changed our lives.

We have published *Hoovering the Roof* to celebrate over a decade of local creativity with you.

Learn more about EDWG, and comment on the anthology via our website at edwg.co.uk

Contents

Contents

Les Tournesols RICHARD WOODHOUSE

'What's up with Papi?' Beatrice asked after lunch.

Father pulled at his beard.

'Bah, he's just being Papi.'

At nine years old, Beatrice didn't really understand this explanation but her father was already on his way to the kitchen, so she picked a crumb of bread off the table, popped it in her mouth and walked out into the hot, dusty air. By the time she had called for Bruno, Beatrice had forgotten all about Papi. The girl and her Labrador wandered the parched French countryside around the family farm all afternoon: catching butterflies, chasing rabbits and throwing stones until, hot and thirsty, it was time for them to return home.

Beatrice jumped over the stream that trickled through the valley and ambled up the lane with Bruno panting by her side. At the top of the rise the dog began to bark then scampered off. She called after him. It was too late: he had dived though a hedge and was gone. Grumbling, Beatrice clambered through after him into one of their sunflower fields. The plants shone into her eyes like spot lamps. Squinting around the field she spotted her grandfather sitting beneath the old ash tree on a stool, with Bruno lying at his feet. She brushed wayward blonde tresses from her face and sauntered over.

'Why you sitting here, Papi?'

He scratched his pitted nose. 'Just waiting.'

'For what?'

'For them.' He jabbed a thumb at the sunflowers.

Beatrice surveyed the parade of flowers and tried to understand what the old man meant. She disliked not knowing things and often pretended to know more than she did. Sometimes she even got away with it – but never with Papi.

'I've been growing sunflowers all my life,' he explained in his deep dark forest of a voice, 'and yet only yesterday did I realise something mighty odd. I was looking at Crow Field.' He turned and gazed at a field on the further side of the dirt track that led from their farm. 'You notice anything, Bea?' She looked hard but saw nothing and said as much. 'What do you know about sunflowers, girl?'

'You can eat the seeds or make them into oil.'

'True.' He patted Bruno's rump. 'But why are they called sunflowers?'

She flicked a fly buzzing around her ear. 'Because they look like little suns?'

'Well, maybe. But also 'cos they like to follow the sun.'

'Oh, yes.' She put her palms about her face like petals and performed such a charming sunflower mime it made the old man chuckle.

'Look at Crow Field again, little one.' She looked. 'Now look at this field.'

She compared the two back and forth until in a flash it came. 'They're looking in different directions. This field's

2

looking at the sun, the other's not. Why's that, Papi? Are they dead?'

'No, they're just getting old – like me.'

She had been surrounded by sunflowers all her life, yet it was only now their inevitable death struck her as unfair. Something so beautiful and so full of life should never have to die. Looking at her Papi, with his leathery skin and marble eyes, Beatrice was filled with such a confusion of love and loss that she had to turn away from him.

Papi took hold of her chin and turned it back. 'We all got to go sometime. Can't grow a new crop without getting rid of the old one, now can you?' She shook her head. 'Anyway, there's something far more mysterious going on here than death.'

'There is?'

'Can't put it into words but you can feel it in here.' He took his hand from her chin and touched his solar plexus. 'And I see it in them flowers. In the way they're all facing the same way.'

'Why?'

'Can you not see what all them flowers are saying?'

Beatrice scowled as her brain hummed, then she became annoyed and finally petulant. 'No, I can't. What's it matter anyway? I'm going in for tea.' Off she walked with Bruno in tow.

The old man called after her, 'Don't you see, child, it means they all stopped turning at the same time.'

Bea stopped and turned. 'So?'

'So why would they do that? How would they do that?'

'You planted them all the same time, that's why.'

'Is everyone born on your birthday going to stop growing on the same day?'

'People aren't plants.' She was enjoying the banter now and started retracing her steps. Bruno whined.

'Plants don't do it neither. Look at them, Bea.' Papi was animated. 'Over a thousand plants deciding to stop moving at the same time. Can't you feel the mystery in that?'

It was odd, but she was too hungry to ponder any longer. 'Come on, Papi, let's go in for tea.'

'You go. I'm staying 'til this field stops turning.'

Beatrice and Bruno raced along the edge of the radiant flowers, out into the lane past the duck pond and into the house with a bang. She stole a piece of baguette from the kitchen but got caught and had to set the table. Soon, they were all sitting about the table tucking in to bowls of chicken and flageolet. All, that is, bar one.

'Where's Papi?' Mother asked.

Beatrice stopped chewing and said, 'He's watching sun-flowers.'

Father put his knife to attention. 'He's what?'

'Watching sunflowers in Upper Field.'

'What on earth for?'

'He's got a notion, like you said. Something about waiting for them flowers to stop their moving.' Disinclined to elaborate, she picked up a drumstick and stuffed it into her mouth. Father looked at Mother. She raised her eyebrows. With a sigh, Father lowered his cutlery and walked over to the window. A buttery evening sun shone onto his bony face. He looked at Upper Field and saw his father's silhouette sitting under the old dead ash tree. Shaking his head, he returned to the table.

4

'Are you not going to get him, Raymond?' Mother asked.

'I've had enough of him, Marie.'

Nothing more was said about Papi. Beatrice wanted to press her mother about what was going on, but kept quiet. After supper, Beatrice scampered to her room, jumped on the bed and stared out the window. The setting sun was blood orange. And there, in a sea of burning flowers, hunched on his milking stool, was Papi. She watched his still figure for a while. He looked like a standing-stone.

Beatrice leapt off her bed and ran down the stairs and into the kitchen. Making sure no one was watching, she wrapped two chicken pieces in a chequered napkin then ran to the door.

'Where you going, little lady?' Marie peeked around her wingback chair. Suddenly bashful, Beatrice announced she was going for a walk.

'Why don't you go and see Papi? See if you can encourage him to come home?'

'Uh, okay, Mama.' She opened the door.

'He might like some chicken – if you've a mind to take it.'

'Oh, he'll be alright,' Bea said, her face reddening. She flew out of the house. Marie returned to her lace with a wry smile.

The sky had turned lavender and the clouds tangerine.

'You staying out here all night?' Bea demanded as she approached Papi. He didn't answer. It was only when she was standing right beside him that he woke from his reverie.

'Oh, hello, Bea.'

'I brought you some chicken.' She handed over the napkin.

He chuckled and patted her head. 'Thank you.'

'Papi, are you really going to stay out here all night?'

'Have to, they might stop their turning.'

'Oh, they don't move at night, it's dark.'

'That's what I always supposed.' He tilted his head close to her ear. 'But I've realised something; them sunflowers in Crow Field aren't facing West where the sun goes down, but East where it rises.'

Her eyes widened. 'So they must have turned at night.'

'Or they woke up one morning and turned to the rising sun – then stopped.'

'That don't make sense.'

'It sure don't. That's why I'm here for the duration.'

'Can I stay with you?'

He laughed. 'What do you think Raymond would say to that, missy?' She pulled a sour face. 'That's right. Anyway you've an important job now – getting me food.' He bit into his chicken and they grinned conspiratorially.

The following morning, Beatrice looked out of her window as the early sunlight cast its tawny hue across the land. The rooster preened on top of the barn, the ducks pecked about the lily pond, the piglets suckled at the sow and young Bruno sniffed around the farm gate. Everything was as it always was. But in Upper Field ghostly wisps of mist hung around the sunflowers. And there, rooted and as resolute as the great ash he sat beneath, was Papi.

'That stupid old man will catch his death,' Father said as he battered the shell of his boiled egg.

'He's not stupid,' Beatrice said.

'Now don't you start getting any notions too, my girl. Notions don't feed the animals, notions don't thresh the crops.'

Beatrice's backchat was halted by Mother demanding from the kitchen what Bea wanted for breakfast. Her hot chocolate, bread and raspberry jam disappeared in an instant.

'Finished,' she announced, grabbing a croissant and running out the house. Her father's voice chased at her heels, demanding to know when her chores would be done – but she was gone.

Beatrice ran up the hill to the moist sunflowers and Papi.

'Morning, missy.'

'Papa's really annoyed with you.'

'There's a surprise.'

She perched on his knee and leant against his chest. He put his arms around her. She could feel the damp and cold of him seeping into her, but she didn't mind.

'Why does he get so mad with you?'

'When you're young you can act irresponsible and no one gives a damn -'

'Like me?'

'Like you. But when you gets older, people rely on you and then everyone gives a damn.'

'So you have to be responsible.'

'Exactly. But when you get older still -'

'Like you?'

'Like me. Then you begin to realise what's really important in life and you start acting irresponsible all over again. And no one gives a damn again.'

'Except Papa'

'Ah well your Papa's your Papa.'

Papi gave Beatrice a wink but she could not grasp its meaning.

'I brought you a croissant,' she said, holding it up.

'Clever girl.'

'Sorry it's only one.'

'Don't fret, I've got some saucisson in my bag.'

'What are the flowers doing?'

'Moving.'

'So they didn't stop last night.'

'No, perhaps today.'

'I'll stay and watch them with you.'

'I'd love that, Bea, but your father's annoyed with me enough. Go and do your chores and come by later.' He pushed her off his knee. She pouted her shiny lips. 'Go on, the quicker you do them, the quicker you'll be back.'

She dragged her feet for a few steps then took off like a hare along the field back to the house and set about her tasks with gusto. There were eggs to collect, animals to feed, boots to be cleaned, and much, much more. Raymond was so pleased to see Beatrice going about her tasks with purpose that he invited her on a trip into town after lunch for a treat.

In the way of the young, with their hearts empty of empathy or artifice, Beatrice spoke her mind. 'I don't want to go into town. I want to watch the sunflowers with Papi.' If she had been looking at her father's face, instead of the dead ash tree, she would have seen it contort with the pain.

'I don't want you wasting your time on foolishness.'

'It isn't foolishness. Papi wants to know when the sunflowers stop moving, so do I.'

'What does it matter? Look, Beatrice, it's the school holidays, you should be spending time with your friends, not a simple old man.'

'Why don't you like Papi?'

He was taken aback. At two metres, Raymond may have towered above his daughter, yet at that precise moment she could have knocked him off his size forty-sevens with ease.

'It's not a question of like or dislike,' he said almost to himself. Then, raising his arms into the air, he bellowed, 'This farm does not run itself! If you don't want to come to town

8

fine, but I'll not have you listening to that old fool either. After lunch you'll help your mother.'

Beatrice put on her best sulk throughout the meal but it was all to no avail. Father went to town and she ended up in the kitchen. As it happened, Bea had a nice afternoon with her mother. They even baked her favourite – lemon drizzle cake. Even so, she couldn't help thinking about Papi and his sunflowers. Whenever possible she would look out a window to his bent figure, hoping the sunflowers were still turning.

When her duties were finally done, Beatrice asked her mother if she could visit Papi and held her breath for nearly a minute before eventually hearing – yes. She ran out of the kitchen with a holler, leaving her mother chewing her lip and worrying her apron strings

In the yard, she was joined by an excited Bruno and they chased along the track toward Upper Field. Papi heard their commotion and decided to stretch his legs by walking to the gate to greet them. Bea leapt into his arms and they laughed, Bruno barking around them. Papi suggested they walk around the sunflower field and talk.

Beatrice explained why she had not visited him and he tutted sympathetically. She promised him a slice of her cake and he licked his lips. Papi told her about all the things he had seen in the field – as well as a few he had not seen and she was filled with wonder.

When the sniffing dog, skipping girl and striding old man turned the final corner of the field, they saw the tall figure of Father standing under the ash.

'I told you to stay away from this field, young lady.'

'Away from me, you mean.'

'I'm talking to my daughter.'

'Mama said I could.'

'I don't care what she said; you knew my wishes well enough.'

'Calm yourself.'

'How can I stay calm when you seem intent on filling my daughter's mind with all manner of foolishness? I work every hour the Lord sends to keep this damn farm going. And what do you do? Stare at sunflowers!'

'Don't you question my loyalty to this land, boy. I've shed more tears, sweat and blood into this soil than you ever had to.'

Father grabbed Bea's arm. 'Come back to the house.'

'Don't take it out on her.'

He dragged her away.

'This farm may need tending,' Papi shouted after him, 'but so does your life, son.'

Father burst into the house as Mother was setting table. 'I'm sick and tired of this family,' he shouted. 'This place could go to the dogs and none of you would give a damn.'

'Go and wash your hands, Bea.'

'Did you say she could see that old fool, Marie?'

'He's her grandfather; you can't stop their relationship because yours is in ruin.'

'That man would have you both turn against me.'

'No one's against you.'

'Ahh, I may as well set a match to the whole place and jump on top.' He grabbed his straw hat and strode past her. 'I'm off to the bar.'

'But your dinner, Raymond?'

The door slammed. Tension hung in the air like a noose. Beatrice and her mother ate their liver in silence. When all was washed and put away, Marie picked up her lace and Beatrice went to her room. She tried to read but anxiety troubled her. Throwing her book down, she stared out of the window. Papi had become nothing more than a shadow beneath a starry sky. Beatrice tried to watch him but her eyelids grew heavier and heavier. Finally, she succumbed to fatigue and slumped on to her pillow.

She was fast asleep when Raymond's truck careered down the track and skidded to a halt in the yard. Raymond got out, meandered to the front step then stopped – his mind wavering as much as his torso. He scratched his beard, wiped the dome of his head and finally turned on his heels, only to totter then fall. Cursing, he stood and breathed in the clammy air and then stomped his boots across the yard. Bruno barked at him.

Shrouded in the night's fragile hush, Papi listened to the barking and heard the angry boots approach. He opened his flask of brandy and took a swig. The pain in his stiff knees made him groan when he stood. Under the silver light of the moon, the sunflowers had turned into rusty chrome shower-heads. Unblinking, he watched his drunken son enter the field. Papi put his flask away. The angry boots marched along the ranks of flowers right up to him. The two generations glared at each other – the elder half-expecting a punch, the younger half-expecting to throw it.

Instead, Raymond crashed into the wall of sunflowers screaming, and started to break stem after stem and crush flower after flower.

'No, Papa. Papa! No!'

Beatrice, dressed in pyjamas and slippers, ran into the field and tried to grab hold of her father's thrashing hand. It hit her across the forehead and knocked her to the ground.

Bruno bounded up and began to bark. A voice screamed, 'Raymond!'

Panting, he stopped his flailing and turned. It was Marie.

'Have you lost your senses?'

She ran and scooped Beatrice up. Seeing his daughter crying in her arms restored his senses.

'What have I done? What have I done?'

The old man approached, tears in his eyes. 'Oh, Raymond, Raymond, how have you become so bitter?'

'By having a father like you,' he snarled.

'I only ever did what I thought was best for you.'

'What *you* thought! Not what *I* thought!'

Beatrice wriggled out of her mother's arms and jumped between them.

'Stop fighting, stop fighting, stop fighting,' she ranted, jumping up and down.

Marie took hold of her husband's fist. 'She's right, Raymond. It's enough.' She prised her fingers between his. 'Papi, the fighting has to stop.'

Papi looked at her and nodded.

'You're a good farmer, son. You've turned this place around.'

'I don't give a damn about the farm! I don't want to be a farmer. I never wanted to be a farmer.' Raymond dropped to his knees. 'I wanted to be an engineer.'

Face full of concern, Beatrice looked to her mother. Marie offered her a hand of reassurance and she took it.

The old man knelt and put an arm around his son. 'I didn't want to be a farmer either,' he confessed.

Raymond's lost eyes looked shocked.

'It's true, son. I wanted to be a pilot.'

Raymond shook his head in disbelief. 'A pilot? You never told me that.'

His father sighed. 'When the war came, I enlisted into the Air Force. But I was colour-blind. And that was that.' Papi gave a sad smile.

'So that's why you joined the Army.'

'Yes, son. And I tell you, after the horrors I endured I was more than glad to return here and be a farmer. It was what I was born to do. It's like these flowers.' He pointed a thumb around him. 'They spend all their days watching the sun, wishing they could be like her. Then one day, they get up and realise their roots are never going to leave the ground. So they stop chasing crazy dreams and become what they really are – wonderful flowers.'

Raymond looked at the destruction he had caused and bowed his head in shame.

Papi chuckled. 'You're only a small hurricane. There's plenty more of them flowers left.'

Raymond helped the old man stand.

'You never told me growing up would be so hard.'

'Sure I did, but you never listened – the young never do.'

'I am so sorry.'

Papi hugged his son and Raymond hugged his father. Then Marie and Beatrice hugged them both and with smiles on their faces they all cried.

At last Papi stepped back and advised, 'You had all better turn in, it's very late.'

'Oh no, we're going nowhere,' said Marie. 'Not 'til these flowers stop turning. Are we, Bea?'

'No way.'

Papi shrugged and Marie and Beatrice went and got blankets. Bruno and the four of them then huddled together in the dark under the dead ash until the stars and the planets and the moon had dissolved into the dawning light. By and by, the sky became a shimmering blue and the sunflowers giant lemon-pops. Insects crawled, birds flew, reptiles slithered and animals scampered. Then gently, oh so very gently, the field of sunflowers began to stir. Degree by degree, each dew-covered head began to turn its face to the burning orange ball in the East. But would they follow it back to the West? That was the question. Beatrice, Papi, Marie and Raymond barely dared breathe as they watched the earth turn and the sun rise. Inch-by-inch, mile-by-mile, it became clearer and clearer that, yes this was indeed the fateful morning the sunflowers would cease their sun worship. Its heat radiated down on them but the flowers shunned its warmth. An energy entered the field so subtle and fine the universe seemed to pause. The silence was profound. And for a few sacred moments, four people breathed in eternity and each knew exactly where they wanted to be.

Bruno couldn't understand what all the fuss was about because he had always known **exactly** where he wanted to be – with Beatrice.

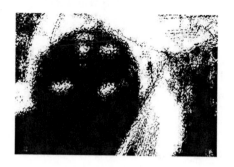

A New Beginning   MARK KIELY

Two years ago. Five-thirty on a Friday evening. Bright summer sunshine. The entrance to Warren Street underground station. A young man and woman stand facing each other on the pavement.

'After all that's happened! You really expect me to forgive you?' She flung the words at me like shrapnel.

'I'm sorry. A thousand times... I'm sorry.' I was struggling to find the right words and already understood the futility of my task.

'Sorry doesn't matter. Sorry doesn't mean a thing.'

'What about if I say I love you and I always have?'

'Shut up.' Her tongue danced sadly upon these two short syllables.

I wanted to tell her that the last six months meant more to me than the previous thirty-three years of my life. Perhaps she knew this already. But I had betrayed her, and she could no longer bring herself to believe me when I told her of my love.

There was anger in her eyes when they fixed upon me. When they drifted from one passer-by to the next, there was hopelessness.

15

'Goodbye, Max.' She turned and walked away.

I watched as she was engulfed by the crowd endlessly milling down into the depths of the Northern and Victoria Lines.

My knees smacked the paving stones as, falling forwards, my legs gave way beneath me. I could have carried on standing, but what was the point? I had spent too long on my feet. What else was there? I could not simply walk away from here, putting one foot in front of the other, one foot in front of the other. For the rest of my life.

Kneeling on the ground amid the bustle of the West End rush hour, I raised my arms into the air and screamed. It was a cry born of every joy and every sadness I had ever known. Closing my eyes, I saw my life pass in its entirety, past, present, future – all brushed with a clarity that stemmed from her vision. I had turned right and turned left, had sometimes made the right choice and sometimes not. And then I met her.

I could not open my eyes. Hands still raised, I swayed from side to side. My arms brushed against a leg, but nobody challenged my behaviour. I was alone. Even if somebody had enquired as to my welfare, there was nothing for me to say. What use did I have for words? Words had not enabled me to tell her that I could not live without her. Words had not enabled me to show her that, for both our sakes, we must stay together. Words would not save the lives of the unborn children we would have reared to be happier, kinder, more content than we had ever been. I began to babble at the top of my voice until, reaching down into my lungs and screaming out loud, I brought forth every blasphemy against words that I could find.

A New Beginning

Opening my eyes, I blinked up at the London Transport sign that most of my audience probably assumed I was worshipping. What was I doing? I had to stop her. I had to tell her that, beyond all my idiocy and selfishness, we would always love each other. How?

I rose to my feet. As I took off my jacket and dropped it to the ground, I heard a voice asking me if I was okay. I knew now that I was.

One quick pull on the laces was all that it took to loosen my trainers. I kicked them off. My tee shirt was new and my favourite colour and flying through the air.

'Oh my... what is he doing?'

'He's mad!'

'Quick, see if you can get his trainers...'

My socks meant nothing to me. My belt, my jeans. She was all I needed.

I ran through the entrance of the station. There were ticket-machines in front of me, while my wallet was in my jeans pocket and already halfway to King's Cross. A ticket inspector cautiously approached me. 'Excuse me, sir, but I don't think...' As I skipped past him, I wondered whether he actually intended to finish off his sentence by informing me that I was not suitably attired for this mode of transport.

There was a roar from the other commuters as I shed my boxer shorts and hurdled the ticket-machines.

'The police...'

'Watch out, mate!'

Turning around, I saw two police officers being let through the gate by the ticket inspector. I ran on ahead, weaving through the crowds. As my feet slipped on the smooth surface of the escalator, I strained my eyes to find her. Platform Two.

Southbound. Reaching the bottom, I sprinted through another tunnel and emerged onto the platform as a train appeared out of the tunnel. Was the applause for me or for the eagerly anticipated arrival of the train?

There was no need to slip between the people waiting on the platform. Like the Red Sea, they parted before me. I wanted to hug and thank everyone for their consideration, but my suddenly liberating cognition told me that this might be somewhat distressing for them. The train stopped, and the doors opened. I could not see her anywhere on the platform.

'SARAH!' I had never known a silence like it. Following my imploring cry, the spectators all fell silent and turned to face me, while my feet took root on the spot. Like a well-choreographed chorus-line, the people in front of me took two careful steps forward or backward to reveal the most startled face of all tiptoeing towards me. It was shrouded with a sense of bewilderment that surpassed every reaction I had previously ever produced in another person. She tells me that I imagine the next bit, but I can remember that the aisle of commuters she was passing along began to hum the refrain from 'Are You Lonesome Tonight?'.

As she reached me, her mouth opened. There was no anger or sadness or pain or loss. I was not quite sure what there was. Nothing in our lives had ever prepared us for this moment.

I placed my hand on her cheek and wondered at the touch of her. When she had turned and left me outside the station, she had become insubstantial, something like a dream.

There was a clatter from the far end of the platform. Turning around, I saw the police officers slowing down as they approached me. Looking back at her, in full view of the wall of faces staring out of the stationary train, I asked her. I did not speak the words. My eyes held the question.

She nodded.

There was another spontaneous round of applause as I embraced her. Even as the police gently pulled our lips apart, we were still savouring the sweet taste of each other. Perhaps it was three weeks later that confetti reined down upon us. Yet in my memory, it seems that it was this day. I can still picture the stern-faced police officer taking the box of confetti out from underneath his helmet and gaily showering us with it.

Hoovering the Roof

Dog-Walking in the Park SUE JENNINGS

Thaw:
a quiet glaze over the furze,
the skies dove-coloured and dripping;
sullied snow-boulders, rolled riotously yesterday
now discarded and disintegrating into mud and
grass.

A clear line of sky over the hill gives confidence
a while, and then,
terriers.

Brindled, pied, red?
At speed, all dogs are grey.

Pets as prey.

Hoovering the Roof

Incontinent fear, tangible on the nose;
the snap-snick at heels before the bite
through to blood and bone
and the shaking, shaking.

Flight is fast.
Silent.
It is the spectators' helpless screams,
hands flapping, articulating pain
that freezes the moment
we will replay again, again
over tea and shredded tissue.

Responsible ownership:
a contemporary issue

The Hidden Phases Of Venus KATE ROSE

June 18th, 1861

Late morning I took a cab up West Hill. From the peak I could see, in the distance, throngs of parasols and toppers pouring forth from cabs, broughams and omnibuses, heading toward our sleek new city of metal and glass. Steam rose from the Crystal Palace's Upper Station, and I found my spirits likewise lifting. It seemed possible to believe London's epicentre was finally moving south; shedding old skin for new invention.

My good mood dipped, however, several minutes later when my driver stopped at a dilapidated five bar gate inscribed with the words: 'Hitherwood Hall'. I skimmed Mrs Whitelaw's letter, and told my driver number two, Rock Hill

Road was required. He whipped the horse's rump, and we proceeded down a steep road to a row of labourers' cottages which, though pretty with climbing roses and sunny thatched roofs, were not what I had envisaged.

I told the driver that I would be ready at noon, and was given the somewhat indignant response: 'This hill's not hacceptable for a thru'penny.'

'Very well,' I replied curtly, 'I shall wait at the top.' It was not my fault that my family now had neither horse nor carriage, and I would not be made to feel inferior because of it.

Yet, as the cab turned and the clatter subsided, I realised I had more pressing concerns than a disgruntled driver. What if the painter found my art trifling? What if he found the education of women ridiculous? And what – worse still – if his uncertainties proved just?

Shielding my eyes I inspected the wild garden with its blaze of irises, some dying. The steep incline had distorted the cottage walls so that they appeared to be melting. As I opened a gate, barely wide enough for my skirts, I saw a neighbour observing me, but my 'good morning' as I reached the cottage was said in a manner perhaps too brusque, too formal, for such a place.

'Have to knock hard, wild urchins they are,' said the prying woman.

Knocking as hard as I deemed polite I prayed she would disappear, failing as I was to alert somebody to open a door. Fortunately, upon a much harder rap – grazing my knuckles – an elderly woman (a loyal servant, I presumed) with greying hair and several missing teeth opened the upper half of the door, whilst simultaneously calling over her shoulder, '*Camille?*' without so much as asking my name.

The Hidden Phases of Venus

A child of two, or thereabouts, sat aboard her hip. Not taking her eye from me, she lowered this child to the floor and unbolted the bottom half of the door, revealing another child entwined in her skirts. On the third, '*Camille?*' which was louder and somewhat grating, two more children appeared; the elder in frayed rags, whilst the younger stood not a yard from my hem, wearing no more than the day he was born and, though I averted my eye, no effort was made to conceal him.

I was gestured inside and narrowly avoided a low beam, just managing to stoop at the last moment, much to the children's amusement. First impressions were that the parlour was tiny, not helped by the inordinate number of children. I counted another seven before the hearth, competing at marbles, forming a living, breathing carpet. Aside from a table and two chairs there was no other furniture, but as my eyes adjusted to the dimness, I spotted a canvas besides the window. It was unframed, a small study, and yet I immediately recognised it from the painting *Paradise* I had seen at the Royal Academy last summer.

I crouched level with the winged angel – wings of an eagle not a dove – admiring its god-like indifference; arms opened wide to the repentant figure, considered to be Eve, crouched by its feet. Its unearthly beauty rendered me awestruck.

'*Mademoiselle?*'

I started, momentarily thinking the angel had spoken. Turning sharply (too sharply for such a bodice) my eyes lighted upon a man, no more than five feet tall with a mass of peppery grey hair partly covered by a beret; smock so paint-stained it left one guessing as to its original colour.

'I did not think you would come so soon,' he said in a half-whisper with a cocked smile, bare toes recoiling beneath the frayed edges of his trousers.

Marbles clashed and a cheer rose from the children, rede-fining the tiny dimensions of the room, drowning my somewhat confused, 'So soon?'

'*Enchanté, mademoiselle!*'

The Academy's most esteemed painter, praised by the *Athenaeum* journal for making art that ignored politics, whose depiction of the Napoleonic Wars had rightfully deserved medals from both the Salon in Paris and the Academy in London, took my hand and kissed it whilst I, struggling with my petit bourgeois preconceived ideas, uttered in a whisper, 'How do you do?'

'Your name, mademoiselle, it has gone from my mind?'

'Marianne Hamilton.'

''amilton,' he repeated, craning his neck as if to suck the missing letter from the air. 'But of course!'

In French he begged his children for peace, promising a ride on somebody's donkey, then pulled a pair of socks from his sleeve.

'*Colette, où sont mes chaussures?* These children, they hide my shoes.' He smiled, tugging on the garments.

I was surprised by his ability, like India Rubber, to switch between languages but it dawned upon me that, aside from the study for *Paradise*, there was no easel, no paints, merely a solitary paintbrush redundant amongst the crumb-littered table top.

'*Alors!* Now we drink coffee. Collette, *café, s'il vous plait!*'

Already of the opinion that the visit ought to be less social and more industrious, I said I would happily forgo coffee, pointing out that his maid appeared occupied. In fact, the woman who had opened the door was so involved with dressing a child she appeared not to have heard her employer.

'Maid?' said the painter, sucking the paintbrush, puffing out imaginary smoke. 'That is my wife!'

How silly of me when he had been summoned at the door as 'Camille' and not as 'Monsieur Zeldin'. My cheeks burned feverishly as Monsieur Zeldin's *wife* clucked like a hen and exited the room tailed by several of her brood.

'My humblest apologies, monsieur -'

'A natural enough mistake! Maids open doors. In Chelsea, my maid opened the door and brought coffee too.'

Wary of another *faux pas*, and aware that the disgruntled driver would not wait long, I hastily turned the subject towards tutorage.

'You are here because of the girl?' the painter asked.

I affirmed that I was here because a mutual friend, Miss Whitelaw, pleased with her portrait, had written to inquire whether he might tutor me.

He looked puzzled. 'Are you paying me?'

'Naturally,' I said running a hand over my purse sewn into the seam of my dress.

'You must be shocked by how I live. I do not live like other Royal Academy artists: your Millais, your -'

'How you live is not my business, monsieur.'

'*Non*, but you will only wonder if I do not tell.' He turned to the audience at his feet. 'What are you looking at? Have you not seen a lady before?' He appealed to me with a shrug. 'Their English is bad! *Vite! Allez!*' With that he hit one or two with the paintbrush. As they left, straining to peer over their shoulders, I said, 'You have a wonderful family,' but naturally out of politeness rather than proper assessment.

'They hinder me,' he said with a sigh. 'And I have many hungry mouths to feed. Look how hungry they are!'

It seemed the subject of money must be broached sooner than I had hoped and, alas, sadly uneducated as to the etiquette of paying people, I clumsily recounted Miss Whitelaw's suggestion of a shilling (hoping that she had mentioned it in her letter) adding, 'But if another day is more convenient…'

'No more portraits!'

'Oh monsieur, I do not wish for my portrait to be painted. I am here because -' He silenced me with a wave and I wondered whether this was perhaps a subtle decline of tutorage too? Had Monsieur Zeldin given up painting entirely?

'I hide nothing,' he went on, as if I hadn't spoken. 'A rich man wanted a portrait of his wife. Her husband, he discovers us in a situation of the most terrible imaginings. I was…how you say? Compromised. This man, he was influential. He tells his friends and…' His shrug was heavy. 'Now nobody comes to Camille for portraits. I do what I am paid to do and if a fat lady takes hold of the man painting her, is that my fault?'

Cheeks once more aflame, I urged myself to respond for the sake of my desires. 'You must appeal, monsieur. You cannot allow one man, whoever he may be, to destroy your reputation.' Yet I was beginning to wonder whether he was altogether capable of teaching. Besides, where were we to paint, the scullery, the boudoir?

'Mademoiselle, your society will not listen to a painter, not a French painter. *Peut-être* I return to Paris. But…' He sighed, sweeping an arm about the room. 'Here my children have fields and donkeys, and if I am miserable, they at least are happy.'

'Well,' I said with false cheer, 'if you are to return to France I hope that you will permit a few lessons before you depart.' I also hoped to have engineered the right pitch; pity would seem offensive. Whatever his present situation, Monsieur Zeldin was a great painter and one that I could learn much from. Surely, the situation could benefit us both?

With a sudden wheeze of laughter, he rose from his seat, his eyes dark, shiny with moisture. 'Let us go in search of the light!'

'Your wife, monsieur,' I said, baffled by his sudden change in countenance, 'Is she not preparing coffee?'

'It has stewed for several days. A few more hours will not matter. But – *Colette, où sont mes chaussures?*' And he darted from the room calling his wife's name, moving like a man of twenty though he was perhaps forty.

As I was about to follow, I noticed a pile of letters upon the mantle. They were clearly not my concern and yet – and I recount this with shame – I found myself picking one up. I turned it over and, recognising the seal, assumed it to be from Miss Whitelaw. In fact, five envelopes were written by the same hand and all five seals remained unbroken, but if Monsieur Zeldin had not known of my visit then why was he accommodating me? However, I had no time to ponder such particulars for he began calling my name. I returned the letters to the mantle and ducked into the kitchen, where Madame Zeldin sat darning, no closer to making coffee than she had been ten minutes earlier.

She looked at me with doleful, untrusting eyes and it was hard to imagine that she was once Monsieur Zeldin's muse. Before so many children, before her body had been depleted of its own creative expression, she was the fallen angel in *Paradise*. Now that she was wizened, her beauty was like old parchment compared to the fresh page; furrowed by years and stained by dozens of demanding fingers.

The painter beckoned me into the overgrown yard.

'Where are we going?' I asked.

He stomped down blackberry bushes and motioned to a narrow track beyond. 'To the light, mademoiselle!'

I lifted my skirts, trampling thorns and unhooked bracken from my skirts as butterflies, disturbed from rest, darted before us like fallen petals. The path opened into a grassy clearing where goats grazed and here the painter stopped, wiped his forehead, and declared, 'Sacrifice! Sacrifice!'

He appeared older than I had at first thought. In the sunshine, the lines gorging the skin around his mouth and between his brows were like knife incisions, as if his entire life had been spent either frowning or smiling. He must, I thought, be fifty or more.

'Sacrifice?' I inquired.

'Patient art demands sacrifice. That is how it is if a little piece of one's soul is to be exchanged with the gods for a tiny piece of heaven. You understand?'

'*Je comprends, monsieur.*' But did I understand? Could anybody, unless they had experienced such an exchange? 'I paint for a hobby, monsieur,' I explained. 'Much to my mother's disappointment, I find needlework tedious and am hopeless at the piano. I shall thus suffer very little. My endeavors will be of the earthly kind. My soul will remain…' I yanked a piece of bracken from my skirt, '…intact.'

'I said, sacrifice, not suffer, mademoiselle.'

He set off again, moving between the tethered goats like a sprightly leprechaun. The clearing became a forest. Ahead, squirrels frantically darted for safety. Danger lay in the prominent roots concealed by the fronds of ferns and I trod carefully as my stays pressed vehemently against my chest. Unless we stopped soon I was going to faint. All previous excitement had left me. I realised that foolishness had brought me here – uninvited and unexpected – and only common sense would bring me back.

'My advice, Mademoiselle 'amilton.'

I leant against a tree taking shallow insufficient breaths. 'Your advice, Monsieur Zeldin?' I gasped.

'Your dress. We are going to paint, not dance.'

'Monsieur,' I said reproachfully, 'I confess a walk had not featured in my expectations of a lesson. Pray, how much further must we journey?'

He grinned at me, eyes twinkling with tomfoolery. 'Life is an unknown journey. One never knows what to expect. Only God truly knows.'

The man was a lunatic!

'God and presently you, monsieur,' I reminded him, deciding this was to be a singular visit.

The painter shrugged. 'People always doubt me.' He produced a pipe. 'Do you suppose that is a gift?'

'It is hardly…'

But he had clamped down upon his pipe like a horse to its bit and galloped ahead. I once more followed breathlessly, driven by the terror of losing myself.

'A folly, *non?*' he inquired, when I eventually caught up.

I followed his squint to a copse of trees and saw above the uppermost branches, intersecting a clear and hopeful sky, angular battlements belonging to, so it would seem, a tower. It was tall, built of pale stone, a solitary smirking gargoyle guarding the entrance. Inside, a narrow stone staircase encrusted with all manner of filth spun us around and around. Cooing pigeons seemed to deafen and the wing of a white dove brushed against my cheek. On what might have passed

31

for the second floor, we entered a circular room with two opposing, glassless, windows. There was a chair, a mattress, a table of paints and an easel whose canvas I could not see.

Having brushed down my skirts and rearranged my bonnet, fumbling with the bow I asked, 'What if it rains?', not yet ready to trust this queer little fellow.

'We move into the centre!'

Beyond the window lay the hills of Surrey. Through the other window, beyond the tree tops, lay the silhouetted ruins of Hitherwood Hall.

'You have permission to be here?' I asked, thinking that the folly must belong to the hall.

His shrug was insouciant. 'Who will stop me? The owner of the big house is dead. People steal his roof, his pipes, his windows, but they will not steal a tower.'

I crossed to the easel, taking in the chaotic arrangement of paints, palettes and brushes. My tutor in Italy had once said that the way a genius works was often a disappointment. Thus far, Camille Zeldin had proved no exception. The canvas was large, almost four feet in height and because of its positioning I expected a rolling landscape, but what I saw abruptly humbled me.

'Who was your model?' I implored.

'My imagination.'

For me to say anything was presumptuous – no preposterous! 'It is...' I stammered, '...it is thought provoking...'

'Go on.'

I stepped closer, attempting to quash my fears. 'One wants to know who she is... looking for...is the letter from her captor...a lover?' I took another step, continuing to maunder. 'It is an unfinished story...a beginning chapter. I want to know...' I forced a smile. '...Perhaps a sequel painting is deemed necessary.'

'The critics will call it sentimental rubbish. They will say...' He spoke haughtily, '...the scene takes attention from the quality.'

'But this is not a familiar scene,' I protested, 'It is not Romeo and Juliet. We see only half of your myth. It is a legend you alone have...created, monsieur.'

'She could be you.'

His voice was soft; my breath caught as thorns had previously caught on the fabric of my dress.

'It is,' he said, 'how I knew I was to teach you. A message from God!'

Though the girl leaning out of the tower's window was partly in profile, the resemblance was undeniably obvious: she was my own image.

'I must admit to a certain similarity,' I half-whispered.

'Pah! We are not so unique as we might suppose.' His shrug was dismissive, both hands raised to the roof. '*Voila, mademoiselle,* welcome to my studio!'

Fury coloured my cheeks. Had he not a moment ago alluded to the divine significance of the similarity? Clearly no longer interested in my opinion, the painter began rummaging through a pile of objects I had not earlier noticed, tossing unwanted implements – brushes, newspaper, a stuffed owl – this way and that.

'Ah!' he said as he brushed off dust. 'This will be yours!'

I explained that I possessed my own easel.

'Mademoiselle, you were barely able to carry yourself!'

'I apologise,' I said, knowing my apology came on account of what lay upon the canvas. 'I thought that you were leading me on a wild goose chase.'

'A wild what?'

'I did not imagine you would paint…' I glanced at my image. '…in such a place.'

'An artist must learn to paint anywhere as long as it is without children and animals. Children especially: they play with paints, steal them, eat them. I use paints from Paris. My patron sends them. Brushes – you must bring your own.'

I said I would pay him for his paints.

'And your imagination, mademoiselle? It is good?'

'It is not to the standard of yours, monsieur. I paint flower arrangements and make studies of fruit.'

'And these excite you?'

'Excite, monsieur?'

'What you paint is as important as how you paint.'

'I would find it very difficult to paint as you do…from one's imagination.' I could not keep the mocking tone from my voice; this did not come from his imagination – it was the reflection I saw every day in my looking glass!

'Difficult, but not impossible. But if you require easy, mademoiselle, you must stay at home – help *Maman* arrange flowers.' He retrieved brown paper from beneath the bed and wrapped it around the easel.

'One more thing…' He offered me some chalk. 'I do not judge. Judgment is what you must do. We do not improve if we rely on others to judge for us. We become – how you say? – lazy. Your own judgment is as good as God's judgment. The two are…' He snapped his fingers.

'Synonymous?' I offered.

'The same, mademoiselle. *Alors*, I shall sit in the light and you shall draw me.' He dragged a chair to the sunshine and lifted his boots to the window's ledge. 'Remember, a person who wants honesty has a daguerreotype. Rich men pay for flattery not sincerity. Imagination, mademoiselle, and do not forget -' He entwined his fingers over his smock. '- wake me when you have finished.'

For the first five minutes I was overcome by fright. I adjusted the position of the easel several times, struggling to avert my eye from the girl upon the canvas. I tried to imagine that, if this was a sign from God, what exactly God had meant by it? After a number of false starts, I turned the paper over to recommence. By the time I had completed the outline of the painter's face, he was gently snoring, and I found myself relaxing a little. I noted that Monsieur Zeldin did not use collapsible tubes but stored his paints in bladders. I mixed a small quantity, noting their quality. My *blanc d'argent* at home seemed infinitely inferior – and his blues were the expensive cobalt kind; his Indian Yellow the brightest I had ever seen, not to speak of his brushes which had ebony handles and silver ferrules. By the time I had begun to apply oils to the canvas, I had entered a state of near somnambulism. I no longer heard the crooning pigeons, my tutor's snoring, or indeed the scurrying of small rodents. It seemed my hand moved of its own volition whilst my mind gently drifted, floating as if in a cloudy empyrean. Never, at Avenue House, had I painted so freely.

After an unknown amount of time a gunshot aroused us.

'Angry farmers fire a gun,' said the painter, dropping his boots to the floor.

He inspected the canvas but, as promised, passed no comment. 'Tomorrow you shall continue,' he said gruffly.

I explained I could not come tomorrow, Wednesdays being my mother's At Home, and I was expected to be there. I took two shillings from my skirt – an extra shilling for the paint – which Monsieur Zeldin snatched, from my grasp, neither mentioning the overpayment, nor thanking me for it. Though the light had been splendid and the peace of the tower a blessed relief – when compared to the persistent ringing of the front bell at Avenue House – the adventure, it seemed, had been merely philanthropic, my sacrifice purely financial. How was I to learn from a teacher who refused to pass judgment? It was one thing deceiving Mother that I was 'out visiting', but quite another giving away Aunt Clara's inheritance indiscriminately. There was little sense in returning.

'Tomorrow. I will explain to you light and tone.' The painter cocked his head as if at last assessing my work. I held my breath but when he remained silent I reiterated that tomorrow was inconvenient.

'In the name of ambition, mademoiselle, you must ignore convenience. Life is rarely convenient.'

My fists involuntarily clenched and unclenched. 'As I have explained, monsieur, I paint for pleasure and I confess I do not possess an ounce of ambition.'

It was the truth, was it not? Ambition did not play a part in the dreams I had moments before sleep, dreams in which my paintings were deemed more than mere wall coverings. Ambition was for men. Ambition was a dream in possession of a backbone. Ambition, in the world of toppers and cigars eventually flourished. My dream was but a whim, yet without it, painting at Avenue House would be infinitely duller. Of course the flowers and the fruit no longer thrilled. Excitement came from those small imperfections – the fly, the dry shriveled petal, the spilt water – but, to admit this to anybody would be to part with a piece of my heart.

'*Qu'avez-vous si vous ne dois pas avoir l'ambition?*'

What do you have if you do not have ambition? The words spun in circles inside my head, switching from English to French until a peculiar feeling washed through me like that

36

before the onset of fever. I felt gripped by a sudden power-
lessness; the sense that my actions were not mine. I told
myself, it was mere coincidence my image lay upon Monsieur
Zeldin's canvas, coincidence, nothing more.

'Now, mademoiselle, some *café*!'

A nearby church chimed noon, and I explained my carriage
was waiting; he must enjoy his coffee alone.

'Alone?' he replied, 'You think that I am ever alone in my
house? Until tomorrow, mademoiselle!'

This is Chapter 20 of a completed novel. **The Hidden
Phases of Venus** *spans the 1860s, through the 1920s to
present day, and explores the quest of two women attempting
to reconcile freedom, love and art.*

Hoovering the Roof

A is L EMMA MACKINNON

So here he is. An old man who wears his trousers rolled – if only for cycling. At 50.

Here we are on a birthday trip. Sitting on the Spanish Steps suddenly burning under the same unfiltered sun as Caesar, Caligula, Hadrian, Nero... and all those other bling covered fated genius nutcase despots. Huge, everything. The legacy of their egos is still astounding. In the Colosseum, Russell Crowe winces as metal clashes and glints. He squints at the soft robed Emperor. He wrestles with tigers.

Gods have been carved. Saints have been carved. The gods, decorated by Christianity, have become saints. Writhing on the banks of the Tiber, a mess of Tritons, sea gods and odd-looking fish. In St Peter's, in a space really nearly as big and planned as some people's kitchens round here, shrouded Madonnas lean out of the dusk. Living liquid marble billowing like silk.

Hoovering the Roof

High Renaissance nonsense cascades in a gold swarm of cherubs from Bernini's altarpiece. Everywhere, bluish stained glass light. Candles illuminate a row of Popes. The priest emerges from the multi lingual confession box, choking on his dog collar.... the nun in supplication, palms clasped, slyly checks her BlackBerry. Emails from Jesus. A trillion years of religious hysteria. You could cut the air with a candelabra.

Scorched and blistered, we pour water on our heads in the shade of another stone church. Traffic hums around the piazza. Richard Scarry mousemobiles. Scooters appear from nowhere, rumbling trivially over the tarmac skin of doomed, buried civilisation. How could you even wield a hammer in this heat – let alone conquer continents?

It's a short trip but cold beers and pizza are swallowed as the world turns on its axis and A contemplates his miniscule previous five decades – and those yet to come.

Enclosed within the Colosseum's arches, vaulted like the dead sockets of a gladiator's skull, we reflect on the legacy of those gaudy emperors. Pomposity and amnesia. In the garden of broken columns and climbing weeds, an American woman rests her head on a slab of marble and sleeps.

New York Boots   AMY GRIGGS

Izzy and I became friends the day we met, in our first weekend at university. She was a bubbly strawberry blonde who
saw past my shy awkwardness and immediately invited me to
go punting with a group of her friends.

Izzy always seemed to have friends, even then, when just
about no-one knew anybody else – her easy temper and infec-
tious giggling attracted people.

Anyway, on that September afternoon we sat by the river
long after the others had returned to halls, drinking a bottle of
sparkling rosé and eating cherries from a basket. It was the
first time I'd ever tasted rosé before – my parents being more
a glass of sherry before dinner and a bottle of Sauvignon
Blanc on a Sunday kind of people – but sitting drowsy in the
sun I remember thinking it tasted like honey; a drink of the
gods. I don't know what we talked about, but I do remember
how she made me feel – like everything I said was interesting
or funny and, buoyed by my own success, I opened up more
and found I could tell her stories in such a way that she laughed out loud. By the time the sun was setting over the Cam, we
were best friends.

Hoovering the Roof

Some nights in the summer we'd lie by the river, chatting 'til dawn. Her father had died when she was nine and her mother – a TV producer – had moved them back to her native Yorkshire and remarried. Izzy didn't talk much about her father, but I got the feeling she felt a little like a visitor at home – a stranger looking through a window into other people's lives. Whatever the reason, she always seemed keen to stay with me in London during the long holidays.

These were crazy days – Izzy always knew the wildest parties to go to and if I'd picked ten people at random in the room she probably could have introduced me to nine of them. Once, we met up with a film director from Ireland and the next day we were flying out to the Galway Film Fleadh. Here, we mingled with actors and directors, artists and musicians, and drank creamy pints of Guinness in pubs painted on the outside like fairytale houses.

At school I'd always hung around with a group of friends, one among many, but for the first time in my life I had a soulmate. Although we had other friends and, at various times, boyfriends, no-one else really came close. I felt like I came alive when I was with Izzy.

After our final exams we spent one last sun-kissed summer in Cambridge. Working as guides we led gaggles of tourists through the ancient colleges and quads, revealing anecdotes and legends as we went. For two short months we shared our Cambridge with outsiders. Perhaps in some small way we were leaving a legacy, as though our stories too must be told or lost forever.

On the last day, we wandered through the deserted corridors of our college, our fingers trailing over brittle walls ingrained with the history of centuries past. At the door, Izzy turned, one hand on the latch, and shouted: 'Hey! Rachel and Izzy were here!' Her voice bounced off the walls and for a second it seemed the voices of students past and future were echoing back and forth across time. Then the moment passed, and we were alone again. Opening the door we stepped out into the sunlight for the final time and re-entered the everyday world.

The everyday world, in this case, was London. Izzy had been offered a job at Dulwich Picture Gallery and I'd found a position as an editorial assistant at a legal publishing firm.

Before her job started, Izzy decided to make a flying visit to New York – allegedly to see some distant relatives, although I suspect the lure of Macy's and Bloomingdale's had more to do with it. She invited me to go with her, but as my bank balance was significantly less healthy than hers, we agreed that I'd stay behind and find us somewhere to live.

After a couple of days trawling around South East London, I finally settled on a terrace house with a roof garden and bay windows. I'll always remember the day she came back from New York, high from the excitement of her trip; the places she'd been, the people she'd met, and of course the clothes she'd bought. She skipped from room to room, each time commenting on something more enthusiastically than the last.

'It's fantastic, Rach – look at all this light! I think there's so much we can do with this place – well done you!' She spun me around, bubbling with excitement in a pair of New York boots – black leather knee-highs with swirls of velvet running down each side.

'I love it! It's going to be brilliant living here!'

Later that evening, over a bottle of rosé, she told me she'd met this amazing guy on the flight back from New York.

'His name's Giorgio – he's half Italian. Gorgeous Giorgio,' she giggled. 'Oh, Rach, I'm in love!'

I threw a cushion at her. 'There's no such thing as love at first sight, Missus!'

'Talk about last of the great romantics! I know you don't believe that really. Anyway, it isn't love at first sight, for your information we talked for five hours non-stop.'

'Lucky person sitting next to you.'

'Oh honestly!' She threw the cushion back at me.

At the time I laughed at her, but I think even then I felt the first stirrings of unease. I'd never really been in love before, and to be honest I don't think Izzy had either. Oh, we'd both been out with plenty of guys, but that's not the same thing at all. Or, perhaps what I really mean is that we'd only ever been in love with each other, and I suddenly became very scared I was going to lose my best friend.

Giorgio, it turned out, also lived in London and within a short time he and Izzy were inseparable. Although he didn't live with us, Giorgio was here so much that on my grumpier days I felt like charging him rent. Sometimes I felt a pang when I came home to find them giggling on the sofa together, but to be fair they always included me in their plans and didn't make me feel in the way. When I'd had a bad day and needed some TLC, Izzy would take one look at my face, dispatch Giorgio off to one of his mates' houses and we'd curl up on the sofa with a glass of wine and a good movie, like the old days.

Anyway, I couldn't not like Giorgio – he was funny and charming, rode a Harley Davidson and most of all was obviously head over heels in love with Izzy. Sometimes I'd invite home a friend from work who I knew fancied me – and although I wasn't quite as in to him, he was good company and we had some fun evenings as a four; cooking dinner and chatting over bottles of wine about old movies, places we wanted to visit and things we'd do if money was no object.

Life was not always completely happy, but never dull. I loved living with Izzy. I loved the way I'd come home from work and could tell exactly what mood she was in from the position of her New York boots. If they were pushed neatly against the wall, it meant she was feeling relaxed, had taken a long bath and was now in the kitchen – glass of wine on the side – calmly preparing dinner.

If – as was more usually the case – one boot was bent over at a rakish angle, it was a sign she was rushing about the house like a mad woman, getting ready for some whirlwind night out. Occasionally, when she'd had a bad day at work or she and Giorgio had had a row, I'd find one boot slung across the hallway (and once, memorably, in the living room). But rows didn't happen very often, and always resulted in a sheepish ring on the doorbell and a huge bunch of tulips – Izzy's favourite flower.

Then one day everything changed. I had the day off and was halfway through a lazy mid-morning bowl of cereal when the telephone sprang into life.

'Rachel...can you come? It's Giorgio … '

'Izzy? What's up? Where are you? You're scaring me.'

'I'm at St George's, Giorgio's been knocked off his bike – I don't know if he's going to be okay, I don't know …'

'Okay, it's okay Iz I'm leaving now, it's going to be okay,' I repeated as though 'okay' was the only word left in the world.

Discarding the remains of my breakfast, I ran to the car, one shoe on, the other perched precariously on the seat beside me. I suppose I intended some mad dash to the hospital but fate, it seemed, had other ideas and within five minutes I was embroiled in a South London snarl-up. Tapping my fingers on the steering wheel I tried all the usual tricks to keep calm. '100, 99, 98...' The bus in front of me moved forward a metre and stopped, blocked by a van coming the other way. I glanced at my watch. '57, 56, 55, for the love of God, MOVE!' Oblivious to my frustration, the van reversed back like a confused snail, inch upon painstaking inch.

The minute the road was clear enough I put my foot on the gas and sped forward, clipping wing-mirrors willy-nilly as I went. At the hospital, I parked without straightening up, pounded across the asphalt and arrived at the front desk of A&E, gasping for breath. 'He'll be okay,' I kept telling myself. 'Bad things don't happen to people you know.'

Summoned by the receptionist, a nurse approached me. She was small and plump with frizzy red hair and a freckle on the side of her nose. I tried to read her expression, but her face was inscrutable.

'Are you a relative of Mr Alexander?'

'No, I'm a friend of his girlfriend. Isobel Woods? She called me. I got stuck in a traffic jam...'

'Okay, you'd better come this way.' She took me to one side and sat me down on an orange plastic chair with a smudged handprint halfway up the back. When she laid her hand on my arm, I knew. My hands started to shake, keys slipping to the floor.

'I'm really sorry, but Mr Alexander died about ten minutes ago. Your friend's in the relatives' room, she's going to need a lot of support right now.'

I nodded, unable to speak. I felt sick and dizzy – and confused: he'd been sitting in the kitchen that morning drinking coffee and joking with Izzy over whose turn it was to do the washing-up. How could he be dead? It didn't make sense.

'Would you like to have a few moments or see your friend now?' I wiped my eyes, tried to pull myself together.

'Now, please,' I replied, although actually that wasn't how I was feeling at all.

I found her in the sterile relatives' room that seemed to seep sadness from every crumbling hole in the wall. She looked so small, hunched down in a chair, half swallowed up by her boots. I put my arms round her. What else could I do?

She was silent on the journey back, her face a blank canvas. At home, she unzipped one boot, then the other, slowly pulling them off her feet. She placed them neatly on the shoe shelf in the hall cupboard and closed the door. 'I'm so tired,' she said. 'I'm going for a lie down.' Later, I heard music coming from under her locked door. It was a CD Giorgio had made for her. I paused on the landing for a second, then turned away. Any intrusion, I felt, would be unwelcome.

I wasn't sure what to expect in the days that followed. Tears, perhaps. Anger even. What I had not anticipated was coming downstairs the morning after the accident to find Izzy scrubbing out the kitchen cupboards and humming Lily Allen songs.

'These cupboards are filthy, Rach, it must be months since we cleaned them.'

'I guess. Do you want a hand?'

'No, it's okay,' she said, turning back to the cupboard. I hovered a few moments longer, wanting to help but not knowing how.

For the next few days – in fact up until the funeral – she was a frenzy of activity: meeting Giorgio's family, helping with arrangements, contacting friends. Then afterwards she seemed to collapse in on herself. She spent more and more time locked away in her room playing the CD over and over until it started to jump in places. Occasionally, she'd emerge for a packet of biscuits or glass of water, then retreat back to the safety of her room. I tried to cook her dinner, but the plates I left outside her door were always untouched an hour later. Before long, she began to resemble a ghost herself – or a sleepwalker unable to wake up from a nightmare.

I'd called Izzy's boss who'd given her compassionate leave, but that couldn't go on indefinitely. He wanted to know when I thought she'd be back, and I honestly didn't know what to say. In the past we'd shared everything, but pain seemed to have replaced her need for friendship. I didn't know how to reach her anymore.

New York Boots

Work became a kind of escape for me. I hated leaving Izzy alone, but I also felt an enormous sense of relief each morning as I pulled the front door shut behind me and re-entered the real world. I know I should have done something sooner – called a doctor, or let her mum know just how bad things were getting – but we'd always handled things together and I thought if I gave her time she'd open up and talk to me. Contacting her family behind her back seemed like a betrayal of trust. It was stupid of course, but anyone can be wise with the benefit of hindsight.

About three weeks after the funeral, I left the house at half seven as usual. I was almost at the station when I realised I'd left the pages I'd been proofreading the night before on the kitchen table. Swearing under my breath, I sprinted back up the road.

As soon as I opened the front door I knew something was wrong. Broken glass lay in the hallway and in the kitchen, cupboard doors were flung open, their contents strewn across the floor. Burglars, I thought – then upstairs I heard running water and the sound of stifled sobs. Something in my brain clicked into place.

Dropping my bag on the floor I ran up the stairs, two at a time, my stomach twisted into knots. The bathroom door was ajar and I pushed it open without knocking, terrified of what I was going to find.

Izzy was sitting on the floor, huddled in her dressing gown. Paracetamol capsules lay scattered around her like grotesque pearls from a broken necklace. In her hand was a shard of glass.

Without thinking I grabbed her wrist, shaking it until she dropped the glass in surprise.

'What have you taken?' I screamed. I wanted to shake her, to slap her for being so stupid, so selfish. And I was afraid.

'Nothing. I wanted to, but I couldn't. I couldn't do it. I hate myself. I don't want to live without him. Why can't I do it? Why can't I...?' She threw her arms around me and we were both crying then, one soggy mess on the bathroom floor. And as relieved as I was, a small, selfish part of me couldn't help thinking, 'Why did you have to do this? Why wasn't our friendship enough to live for?'

Of course everything changed then. Izzy's mum came and collected her that afternoon and took her back to Leeds. For as long as I could, I kept Izzy's room vacant in the hope that she would have a rest, get better and come back. By the time the rent had chewed, swallowed and spat out half my savings I admitted defeat. I had to find a new housemate.

The choice was paltry. In the end, I went with an insurance broker called Colin who wore socks with brown sandals and had a laugh like a hyena, but at least he seemed reliable. He was, up to a point – although his laugh set my teeth on edge and he'd wander around the kitchen eating dry toast, leaving a little trail of crumbs behind him.

I tried to call Izzy countless times, but the phone always went straight to voice mail and when I dialed the landline number her mum said she was sleeping. I think she blamed me for what happened, and perhaps she was right to, but it hurt so much. After a few months I stopped calling, but I didn't stop missing her. Without Izzy, life seemed as mundane and grey as the lingering drizzle outside.

New York Boots

But the funny thing is that even at the crappiest of times life goes on and good things happen. Happiness has a habit of sneaking up behind and tapping you on the shoulder just when you least expect it, and that's how it was for me.

First, out of nowhere, I was offered a promotion at work, and a week later Colin told me he was leaving to travel across the Sahara on a camel. With the extra money I'd be earning I worked out I could afford to pay the rent by myself – for a few months at least.

Then, at a party I wasn't even going to go to, I met Andy. He was a lawyer with a cheeky grin and puppy dog eyes – and within twenty minutes I was smitten. In August, I went away to Crete with some friends from school, and at the last minute Andy managed to join us. The holiday was perfect – two weeks spent reading books on the beach, strolling through co-lourful towns, eating moussaka and drinking vibrant cocktails, while the Mediterranean gently caressed the sand in the back-ground.

On the last night, Andy and I slipped away and wandered down to the beach by ourselves. Perching on a rock, I pulled off my sandals and let the warm sand slide between my toes. We must have sat there for an hour or more – my head on his shoulders, his arm round my waist – just listening to the gen-tle breathing of the sea.

Back in London, Andy and I shared a taxi from the airport. As it drew up outside my front door, he pulled me towards him, and whispered something in my ear. Watching the cab drive away, I felt happier than I had in a really long time. Life seemed pretty good right then.

51

Hoovering the Roof

Humming tunelessly, I unlocked the front door. The first thing I noticed was a pull-along suitcase standing in the hallway. And next to it ... a pair of knee-high boots.

Heart in my mouth, I pushed open the living room door, hardly daring to hope. There she was, curled up in the easy chair by the window – a lot thinner and paler, but unquestionably Izzy.

'Rach – you're back. Do you mind? I didn't know you'd be away and I wanted to surprise you. I'm so sorry about everything...' But she never got to finish that sentence because we were already hugging. Anyway, there are some things between friends that don't need to be said.

Later, a bottle and a half of rosé later, she asked if she could move back in. 'My mum's been great, and I get on much better with my step-dad now, but I just want to get my life back together again. Anyway, I think I might be starting to drive them mad,' she grinned.

Not everything has gone back to being the way it was, how could it? Izzy is a lot quieter for a start. Some days she has sad eyes and then I know she's thinking about Giorgio.

She has another job now and has even started going out with someone new, although I think she's taking it slowly. She's not quite as bubbly or crazy as she was. She works longer hours and wears sensible flat shoes for the tube commute. But just sometimes, on special occasions, she puts on her New York boots – and then I know she's going to be okay.

52

Taste HELEN HARDY

A taste of someone lingers.
We never liked the same
things, the same songs, the same singers.
Does it count for anything
that we sometimes hated the same thing?
The taste of someone lingers.

The taste of someone lingers.
Pink's not my colour,
Elvis sings on your cyclamen shower curtain,
mic tight in his fingers,
scent of mildew and loss a power to sting,
The tasteless sometimes lingers.

Hoovering the Roof

The tasteless sometimes lingers.
An ink cartoon of buddha
propped up by six chipped wine glasses,
not one the same as another,
the drinks long gone – the headache never passes,
A taste that somehow lingers.

A taste that somehow lingers.
Waste not the cushion
where it bears your arse-print, waste not this keyboard
Stained by your fingers.
Your taste's all over this place,
on the tip of my tongue,
A taste of someone lingers.

Max and Me RACHAEL DUNLOP

I can't remember exactly when we stopped using the elevator, but it was before the electricity rationing started, so pretty early on. It was Max who pointed out that, with all the apartment building staff gone, it might not be safe. 'You carry a crow bar on you, honey?' he asked as I pushed the call button. 'That thing gets stuck between floors, I don't know who's going to get you out.'

'I'm not walking up fourteen flights of stairs, Max.' He snorted.

'It's only thirteen flights, Red, remember?'

He was right, of course. I thought it was funny, when I first came to Manhattan, to find that no building had a thirteenth floor. Funny ha ha *and* funny peculiar. Because, of course, it was there all the time, we just pretended it wasn't. Straight from the twelfth floor to the fourteenth. Like calling it something else *made* it something else. Like a number could be unlucky. I didn't think it was funny anymore.

A week after we stopped using the elevator, Max helped me move to a lower floor. We went to the Super's office first and pried open the safe where all the apartment keys were kept.

Hoovering the Roof

'Which one do you fancy, honey?' Max asked. 'You want to take the floor above me? It would be nice to be neighbours. I'm an old guy, I could do with a nice young lady like you looking out for me.'

I laughed. We both knew that Max was the one looking out for both of us. Max lifted a fat bunch of keys out of the safe. The fifth floor sounded good to me, not too high, but not too low either. Now it was just Max and me in the building, I could take my pick.

Up on the fifth floor, we scanned the doors, unsure where to start. 'Those end ones are the biggest,' Max said, pointing to the doors at either end of the corridor. 'Family sized.'

I shook my head. 'I don't think I could.'

'No, you're right.' Max agreed. 'Well, I've got a two-bedroom apartment, it's pretty nice. Why not take the one above mine? The layout will be the same. We could say goodnight to each other in Morse code. Tap it out on the pipes.'

I squeezed Max's hand. I knew what he was doing, trying to make this easier, keep the mood light. 'Okay,' I said. 'Sounds like a plan. You got the keys?'

Max opened the door and I let out a long sigh, not realising until then that I had been holding my breath. All the furniture was still there. The cupboards and closets had been cleared out, the floors swept and refrigerator emptied, its door propped open to stop it growing mould. These guys had packed up and cleared out in an orderly fashion before the city was locked down. They had not been culled. 'One in thirteen hundred.' Max said under his breath. I nodded.

When your number came up for the cull, they pretty much picked you up straight away. Everything you owned was taken by the Community Property Department to be recycled, or reused, mostly for energy. Even though there were so many fewer of us now, the rationing was tight.

One person in thirteen hundred. That was the cull target. Leave one person in every thirteen hundred alive and we would survive. The calculations were impossibly complicated, they said. First of all they had to work out how much farmland was still above the water, how many people it could support, how many people were needed to work it. Then there was the infrastructure to consider, or what was left of it, and how much of it we would still need, when we got down to sustainable numbers.

When so many people died in the first flood, hopes were high that the rest of us would be okay. We had all heard the stories about what had happened in other countries. Northern Europe got it first. When the ice melt suddenly accelerated, the sea levels started to rise. Fast. They thought they had years to plan for the floods. But it only took a few months. The authorities did their best, but it was when the food started to run out that things started to get really nasty.

By the time it was our turn, we knew the drill. Most of us were going to die, one way or another: one way being to starve to death, the other to be killed and eaten. The cull made sense. We didn't fight it. But then again, we didn't have a choice.

My new apartment on the fifth floor had some pretty nice furniture in it, so Max and I just brought my personal stuff down from the fourteenth floor. Still, it was early evening already by the time I got everything straightened out. I dragged an easy chair out onto the terrace to watch the sunset.

It's one of the things people don't tell you about New York City, how beautiful the sunsets are. I'd moved into this building in the first place because it faced west. Sitting out on the terrace now, watching the sun go down, I realised that today was one of the two times in the year when the setting sun lined up perfectly with the Manhattan street grid. For the last fifteen minutes of the day, the slowly setting sun filled each cross street, perfectly bracketed by the darkened buildings as they ran from the East River to the Hudson. I could hardly look at it at first, dazzled by the long spiked rays of light split by the high-rises. But then a thin veil of cloud passed over the sun and I could see it, a hot pink orb sliced in half by the edge of the world.

And then it was gone. In the almost complete darkness, I could hear the silence. Before, Manhattan had its own distinctive background noise: behind the sounds of the cars and the people, of the honking cabs and the delivery boys' rattling bicycles, beyond the judder of generators and air conditioners, and further back even than the constant subterranean growl of the subway, the city gave off its own deep bass thrum. And now it was gone.

But here was something new, a smell. From somewhere below me came an aroma I had never smelt before in the city. It was the sharp scent of a freshly lit barbeque. I leaned out over the edge of the terrace. 'Max, what are you doing down there?' Max looked up at me and grinned.

'Found this kettle barbeque down in the basement. The Super probably confiscated it from some idiot who thought it was a good idea to have a barbeque on his terrace.'

'An idiot like you?'

'Don't think fire regulations apply anymore, Red. Grab your meat ration and come on down.'

In that last thick, hot New York summer, Max's barbeques became a weekly fixture. As soon as my meat ration came in on a Friday morning, I would hand it over to Max. From his dwindling supplies he would make up a marinade and use half his week's electricity allowance to chill the meat until evening. The sweet smell of searing meat drifted down the quiet avenue, and more than once I saw passers-by stop and look up. I wondered if they found themselves suddenly thrown back in time by the smell, back to a time when people and food spilled out of the restaurants and into the streets. So great was our plenty, it couldn't be contained.

After we ate (and it didn't take long, as the rations got smaller and smaller), we would sit on the terrace and watch the sun go down. Hot as it was outside, inside it was unbearable. Sometimes we talked about work: every day, we went where we were told, doing what was needed to keep the city ticking over, holding it in readiness for the day when the re-population would begin. But mostly we talked about our lives before the flood.

I told Max how I came to the city straight from the sticks. In my hometown, everyone knew each other. I was looking forward to the anonymity of the big city. The day I moved into the building, the Super told me: 'Three thousand people live in this building. It's like a small town in its own right. Plenty of neighbours, but you don't have to speak to a single one of them if you don't want.'

He barked out a laugh at this, but it was true. Until the cull started, I barely spoke to a single person in the building, and that's the way I liked it. Like most young New Yorkers, my life was lived in the office and on the street, in restaurants and bars. My apartment was just somewhere to sleep and receive mail.

It was when we were lining up to be tagged that I first met Max. He was in front of me, fresh from his office downtown. I say fresh, but the thing I noticed first was the darkening line of sweat around the collar of his expensive looking shirt. The air conditioners were still running, but at reduced rates now. I lifted the hair from the back of my neck in an effort to cool down, and let out a low sigh. Max turned and looked at me:

'Hey, Red, where'd you get that lovely hair? You Irish somewhere down the line?'

I nodded and smiled. I wasn't in the mood for small talk. He looked too old to be making a pass at me, but I couldn't be sure. As we shuffled along, I watched the monitoring board fill up. As each person was tagged with a subcutaneous chip, a corresponding light came up on the large electronic board that had been installed behind the doorman's desk. No one could get in or out of the building without a resident or staff chip. They told us it was for our own safety, they expected crime to be a problem as conditions got worse. We knew better.

After the first cull, about a third of the lights on the monitoring board went out, some in bunches, other singly here and there across the board. Those of us who were left moved quickly past the board on our way through the lobby, heads down. We didn't know whether we were sorry or glad to have been spared. As the number of people in the building dwindled, I started to recognise faces. People started to say hello. But it was too late for making friends. No sooner had I learned someone's name than another light disappeared from the board and they would be gone. Within a few months, it was just Max and me. Two lonely lights side-by-side on the board. And then the culling stopped.

'So, what do you reckon, Red?' Max asked me one Friday night. 'Did we just luck out? Or do they need us for something?' I shrugged.

'Unless you've got some special skills beyond barbequing, I can't see why they'd need an old man like you.' Max kicked my feet off the upturned crate they were resting on.

'Very funny, girly. But seriously ...'

'But seriously, Max, who knows? I think it's just a lottery. When your number's up, it's up.' Max changed the subject.

'I was working down on the East River yesterday,' he said. 'The dams seem to be holding. Levels haven't risen much these past few weeks.'

'Well, that's good.' I said. I didn't say I thought it was because it hadn't rained in a month, because there had been no snow in the winter to melt in the spring and fill the reservoirs. The water levels in the river should be going down. If they were holding steady, it meant the sea level was still rising. Not for the first time I reflected on the irony of it: in the middle of the worst drought on record, it was the water that was killing us.

I glanced over at Max. He had his head tipped back against the back of his chair, his eyes closed. He looked old tonight. I put my hand on his arm.

'I miss them,' he said without opening his eyes. Max's wife and grown-up daughter had been out of town when the lock down came. He hoped they were still alive, but he had no way of knowing. Statistically, of course, it was unlikely. One in thirteen hundred. Max started scratching at the small weal on the side of his neck where the chip had gone in.

'Did you try to get off the island again today, Max?'

'Every day, Red, every day.'

'And?' Max shrugged, then clutched his throat and kicked his legs out in a comical mime of the electrical charge the chip shot into him every time he tried to cross the barrier. I didn't laugh. After a long while, Max spoke again.

61

Hoovering the Roof

'They're lifting the curfew early tomorrow morning, opening the museums before it gets too hot. Escort gets here at five am, if you want to go to the Metropolitan. How about it?'

'Sure,' I said. 'That would be nice.' I drained the dregs of my beer and propped my feet back up on the crate.

It was late morning when the escort dropped us back at the building. We were behind on our weekend chores. 'I'll do the laundry,' I told Max as we crossed the lobby, 'you go do the maintenance rounds.'

'Is there enough electricity left to run the laundry machines this week?'

'I think so. If not, I'll take the laundry down to the East River and beat it against a rock.'

Max laughed. 'I want my clothes cleaner, Red, not dirtier.'

I stopped. Something was different. I turned, retraced my steps.

'Where are you going?' Max followed me. We both saw it at the same time: only one light on the monitoring board, and the escort van still idling outside the building.

I walked up to the board. Only one light on, and it wasn't mine. I glanced over at the door. Through the grimy glass I could see the armed guards getting out of the van.

Max grabbed my arm. 'Run, Red, run,' he whispered in my ear. But there was nowhere to go and he knew it.

'It's okay, Max,' I said. 'My number's up.' I kissed him on the cheek. 'So long, neighbour.' Even as I walked towards the door, I could feel the chip activating, my legs getting heavier, slower. From somewhere very far away, I thought I heard the words:

'So long, Red.'

The Fat Rats of Flatland DANIEL MAITLAND

This is a chapter from an eco ripping yarn called **The Fat Rats of Flatland**. *It's about a bunch of silly rats (the King rats) who are so wrapped up in their possessions that they forget how to enjoy life and how to be good neighbours. They are taught this lesson eventually by a brave boy rat called Barty Button-nose. In this chapter Barty's underground movement is about to be revealed.*

(No. Stop it. Be'ave yerself!)

Chapter 15: Shadows

Barty had a terrible dream as he slept. He dreamt that he and Roundbelly were playing on a big beach by the side of a huge sea – maybe it was the sea where Bigbottom and Prettyeyes went. They were playing in the bright sunshine and having a very nice time indeed, with a bat they had made out of driftwood and a sponge from the sea that was shaped like a ball. Barty was running down the wicket to bowl at his friend, who was laughing and saying something like, *I'm gonna hit you right over the boundary this time, Button-nose, just see if I don't,* when he suddenly stopped in horror. He looked at the sky with the big burning sun, then back down at the ground, then back up at the sun, then at his friend who had dropped the bat and was walking towards him.

'What's wrong?' said Roundbelly, in the dream.

'They've gone,' said Barty.

'Who has?'

'Our shadows.'

Captain Lightfur was waiting in his office at the Palace. He didn't like to be kept waiting and so he was, as usual, in a bit of a bad mood. There was a knock at the door.

'Come in,' he said.

Two rats came in, both dressed completely in black – with black hats and black handkerchiefs round their necks like highwaymen. They seemed to slide in through the door rather than walk and their heads moved quickly from left to right as they checked the room for danger. One of them bent down to look under a chair.

'Oh do stop it,' said Captain Lightfur. 'For goodness sake! There's only me here!'

'Never be too careful, sir,' said one. And his voice was a whisper and he and his companion still cast their eyes around the room. One of them picked up a knife from the Captain's desk that he used to open letters with. He shouldn't have done that.

'Ow,' he said in his secret voice and dropped the knife to rub the bruise on his head from where the Captain had just walloped him.

'Now sit down.'

'Yesssir,' they said together, with an extra S in to make them sound a bit like a snake, sssss.

'Report.'

The Fat Rats of Flatland

The left rat pulled a black book out of a black bag and opened it. It was full of black paper. He peered at it, moving his eyes closer and further away, then passed it to the other one. Who peered at it too, then passed it back with a shrug.

The Captain sighed very loudly before leaning across and pulling the book roughly from the first dark rat. Who started to protest, then wisely changed his mind and said in a small but still secret sounding hiss, 'Think I may have used the wrong pen.'

'Should have used the red one,' said his partner, secretly.

'Should have used the red one,' he agreed, 'Think I used the black one. Pretty hard to read... isn't it, sir?'

The Captain had wanted to be a fisherman when he was a little boy. There were days when he wished he had. This was one of them. He sat for a moment staring at the black writing on the black paper in the black book, and imagined himself out on a lovely lake in the sunshine with his brand new fishing rod and some lovely worms wriggling in a bucket by his feet. Then the thought of the water reminded him of the current problem and he stood up, closed the book, and banged it on both black rats' black snouts.

'Idiots,' he said loudly.

'Ow,' they said secretly

The Captain put the book away. 'Just tell me,' he said.

He picked up a black pen and started writing on white paper (what a good idea) as the two began reporting on what they had witnessed, because of course, as I'm sure you must have guessed, these were the two that followed Barty and the gang when they left the palace with no tea and one medal. These were the shadows.

After a while the Captain stopped writing and put the pen to his snout and started nibbling on the end.

'Mmmm,' he said, his mood improving. 'Very interesting,' he said, standing up and walking to the window to look at the sun going down outside. 'Well done.'

'Thank you, ssir.'

'Now get out.'

The two black rats slid out of the room in the same sneaky way that they had slid in – heads turning either way again for danger, peeking under chairs. One minute they were there, then they were not...

Then they were there again.

'May I have my book back, please?'

Slam. The book flew blackly across the room and banged once more on the snout. Some rats just don't know when to stay gone.

The two black rats slid out of the room in the same sneaky way that they had slid in

Barty woke up. And sat up in his bed very quickly. He had a feeling of danger. Then he remembered his dream and ran out of the room to go and wake his dad. Ten minutes later they were all sitting downstairs at the other end of a dream being told and all looking very serious. Rats take dreams very seriously and believe that they tell us things.

'It's telling us something,' said Bigbottom.

'Yes,' said Prettyeyes, 'But what?'

'Shadows...' said Bigbottom thoughtfully, 'Shadows.... *The shadows are gone.* Hmmm...'

'Oh no,' said Prettyeyes, who like many mums was secretly a tiny bit cleverer than her husband, but normally keep quiet about it in case he got upset.

'What?' said Barty and Bigbottom together, both feeling a bit more worried – and a funny swirling starting in their stomachs.

'We were followed.'

'No!' said Barty.

'Never!' said Bigbottom, who was proud of his skills as a woodsman and hunter and believed that he would have known.

'Yes,' said Prettyeyes. 'From the Palace, I expect. We were followed... Barty saw, but didn't realize that he saw. And the dream had to show it to him.'

'By the eyes of Snarf!' swore Bigbottom. Then he rushed to the cupboard, picked up the big axe he used to chop wood and started towards the door.

His wife placed her hand on his chest to stop him.

'There is no need now, my love,' she said. 'They are gone. That's what else Barty's dream told us. We had shadows, but they are gone.' She got up from her chair and grabbed a big bag and started to rummage in the cupboards, picking up food and coats and underwear and toothbrushes and stuff.

'What are you doing, mum?'

'We must hurry. They have gone. They will be making their report. Then they will be back. We have no time to lose.'

Bigbottom growled deep in his belly and said something that sounded like, *Let 'em.* Then he too began rummaging in cupboards and putting things into bags, aware also that they had many good Groundrats waiting by the water to be collected and housed, and many other good Groundrats waiting for instructions, and that all could be in danger now because of their carelessness. Who knows how much those shadows may have overheard or seen? His one consolation was that there was no way they were in any of the boats – he would swear that he knew every good rat involved in that adventure – so the rats by the water should at least be safe.

Within five minutes they were packed. Bigbottom loaded the bags onto his broad back, picked up his axe, put his wife and child behind him and opened the door.

'Hello,' said Captain Lightfur, who was standing in the doorway. His hand was raised as if about to knock, and twenty soldiers with guns and swords were behind him.

They were too late.

'Run!' shouted Bigbottom, pushing his wife and child back into the kitchen and towards the back door. Then he lifted his axe with a roar like a lion and charged out into the front yard, slamming the door behind him.

'No!' screamed Prettyeyes.

'No!' shouted Barty.

Bang, went a gun.

A Day for Janni SUE JENNINGS

Approaching the top of the hill, Fay stopped to check on her companion's progress.

'How're you doing?'

Tall, stout and rolling from side to side in her laboured engagement with the incline, the other woman made no reply. Her tongue protruded slightly at the right-hand corner of her upper lip. Fay stood still for a moment, taking pleasure in the gentle breeze.

Janni drew level with her, beaming as usual.

'Fiiiine!'

Those elongated Seaford vowels were uplifting and received with as much affection and amusement as ever to Fay, whose flat, Kentish tones were in such direct contrast. Her friend, puffing slightly, placed one hand on her ample hip and ran the other carelessly through short, black, greying hair that stuck up damply away from her face. A once lovely face that even now gave pleasure to others when she spoke as it lit up with animation and interest.

'Ohh, *look*, Fay, how *beautiful*. You can see for *miiiiiles…*'

Fay smiled. She had looked forward to bringing Janni to this part of Kent in May, had been concerned that there wouldn't be time. But Janni was in remission.

Away to the right was the sweep of a golden rape field; to the left, beige barley and, at the entrance to the beech wood, a carpet of bluebells, their rich hue neither really blue, nor yet purple; beautiful enough to be the one sight she remembered and waited upon with longing each year.

'Shall we eat our sandwiches on that bench at the top?'

'Oohh, *shall* we? It's early…Let's! I *do* adore a picnic lunch. What've you brought?'

'Cream cheese and lettuce, cheddar and pickle, or vegetarian pâté with tomato and watercress'.

'*Love*ly. I'll have the cream cheese, if I may – oh, and a pâté as well.'

The two women reached the summit and sat on the bench whose brass plate read:

In Memory of Arthur Handley. He loved this place.

'Why is it that people feel the need to stamp ownership on tiny pieces of the planet through things like this?' Fay was mildly irritated.

'What, names on benches? Yes – there are a lot I suppose.'

'Why?' Fay was warming to her topic.

A Day for Janni

Janni, recovering her breath, chuckled benignly, awaiting the rest of the flow.

'I mean, if his wife and family ever come here, they'll hardly need an etched reminder of Arthur and his love of this hill, will they? They loved *him*, he loved *this*...' She opened both arms in an expansive gesture. 'He'll be *present* whenever they're *here*.'

Fay began to unpack the lunch. 'It happens a lot in *high* places,' she continued, handing Janni her sandwich. 'The cliffs of North Cornwall; the Devon coastline; you come abruptly upon a bench that announces some deceased soul's appreciation of a particular view. Nice in a way – but it's obtrusive, somehow – like a demand for attention where none is really required.'

Janni ate her sandwiches voraciously, exclaiming, as she did so, on their deliciousness, the skill of their maker.

'I don't know *how* you find the time for all you do, Fay, really I don't. You walk the dogs, you ride your bike – then there's the house and the garden... I wish...'

'You've always been such a wonderful socialiser. I never did that. Think of all that value-added interaction you've had while I was cleaning the bloody cooker and bathing the dog.'

Fay was quick to stem any signs of negative retrospection. To her way of thinking, every moment the two friends spent together needed to be gilt-edged. Fay gazed down at the colours spread below them. First narrowing her eyes, she then blinked them hard – tried to imprint the picture somewhere behind their lids. Was that, she wondered, how Impressionism worked? On the 'mind's eye'? Of course, there was ambience, texture, other sensory information. How she'd love to paint. Janni painted. Fay turned to face her friend.

'This is why I love England. Why I stay here despite the fact that it's a ridiculously bloody expensive mickey-take on the consumer. And the householder. And the taxpayer. The honest ones in particular.'

Having toyed with half a sandwich, Fay now peeled an orange, deftly removing the pips and depositing them into an empty Tupperware container. Janni watched her thoughtfully.

'Yyeeess.' A heavy sigh issued from Janni, who had finished off most of the sandwiches and was lighting a cigarette. She drew on the filter tip as though on a long-awaited opiate, half-closing her eyes, her face assuming the blissfully contented expression it always did when she smoked. 'I wish I'd had a child.'

Children. Neither of them had children. Fay had married, disastrously, at twenty-one. He was an older man whom, she'd quickly realised, was not the person her youthful self had naively believed him to be. They had divorced after seventeen unhappy years. Janni never married. She'd had a string of affairs, starting when she was twenty-four, and which culminated in the love of her life: a married man, ten years her senior, who used and abused her for some fifteen years before dying of an aneurism when he was sixty-seven.

'Yeah. Guess I'm the lucky one there. I've had hundreds. And I've never had to change a single nappy.'

They both laughed. Fay had been a teacher for twenty-three years, retiring much earlier than she'd anticipated, after receiving an unexpected and generous legacy from a favourite uncle.

'Just think, Fay, of the inspiration you must have provided for a whole generation!'

A Day for Janni

Fay laughed. 'Desperation in a lot of cases, I would think. It's not always possible to find a taker for the Muse.' Fay's specialism had been creative writing with more challenging groups of teenagers. 'Fruit?' Fay held out the large plastic box to her friend.

'Oh, no, thank you. I really don't...'

'You should, you know.' Fay peeled a banana and began to polish an apple on her jean-clad thigh.

'Can we go shopping again?' Janni asked suddenly. Fay left off tidying the remains of the picnic and leaned back on the bench. She looked closely at Janni, who was staring upward into the arching, blue cathedral of the day. For once, she was still; her hands, usually animated, either gesticulating or occupied with a cigarette, lay upturned in her lap. Fay tried not to see the posture as one of vulnerability, of ultimate helplessness.

'You like that, don't you?'

'I do. You're such fun to shop with, dear girl – you're such a *tart*!'

'Remember those boots?'

They both laughed. There had been one memorable shopping trip when Janni had been looking for boots – sensible, quality, classic boots. Fay had found, to her nostalgic delight, a pair of boots evocative of the early Seventies when, as a young woman, she had been teaching theatre dance. She had held them up before her friend: 'Look – aren't they gorgeous?'. Multi-coloured suede with a six-inch heel, Fay would have felt transformed by those boots. Janni had thought them vulgar, and couldn't refrain from saying so.

Hoovering the Roof

'Oh, Fay, if you wore those to the Crown and Anchor on a Friday night…well, your reputation would be well and truly made. And you'd never need to buy your own drinks!'

They had both laughed heartily, Fay never for a moment feeling offended by her friend's suggestion that she lacked taste and refinement. She knew her upbringing had been firmly rooted in the jet-set '60s, her parents impressionable, under-educated social pretenders. How often she had wished, wickedly, at Bible classes, or at teenage weekend gatherings, that she had been born into a different family, one that might have made her integral, less obviously the accidental conception of two troubled people.

Fay looked thoughtfully at Janni. 'What will you look for this time?'

'Oh, a dress, I think. And a jacket, too, perhaps.'

Janni lived in a small seaside town where everything had an expensive price tag – subtle, hand-written; nestling close to the thick, satin designer label. In those shops, with their thick carpets and hushed can-I-help-yous, the designers were known personally, lived a street or two away. Janni wanted cheap, comfortable, utility clothing. Early on in their friendship, she had marveled at Fay's descriptions of the range of fashionable gear available in her Kentish hometown: 'The benefits capital of the South East', Fay had laughingly defined it. 'If clothes weren't cheap, half of Beechford would be walking around in rags.'

She thought for a moment. 'Right. You say a day. Tell me what colours, styles and so on, and I'll do a reccy beforehand to save a bit of time. New Look are doing a great line in skin-tight snakeskin-print satin.'

A Day for Janni

'Oh, Fay, you *are* a treasure!'

Fay knew that the proposed shopping trip would tire her friend; wanting to provide only positive experiences so far as she was able, she would try to limit the amount of stressful walking and searching by narrowing the field. Restless after sitting, she stood up and stretched, shading her eyes with her hand and looking toward the bluebell wood.

'Ready?' she enquired.

'Oh, *yes.*'

Carefully, they began the descent to the left of the bench leading to the wood. As the well-trodden path disappeared, cobnut cases crunched underfoot and the fresh, faintly acid aroma of the bluebells assailed them. Looking up, Fay experienced the familiar rush of pleasure she always had on seeing the canopy of delicate, green beech leaves overhead. A light wind ruffled them. A million tiny, pale fresh flags to herald the onset of the new summer.

'You know, we're not really supposed to pick them, Fay.' Janni lit yet another cigarette as though it were the first in hours.

Janni's voice was unusually quiet, momentarily devoid of its resonance and expression. Fay turned towards her.

'The day I can't pick a few bluebells in the country, is the day I'll buy a one way ticket to... Ethiopia,' she finished, somewhat lamely. 'Anyway, we only want a few, just to – to remind us of the visit.' Then: 'Janni?' The other woman bent to stub out her cigarette on a large, flat stone.

'Dear Fay!' Janni beamed fondly at her small friend, ready to comply with whatever request she seemed about to issue.

'Would you paint them?'

'The bluebells? Ohh, of course! But … they may not be quite – well, you know – still life'.

Fay smiled broadly, knowing exactly what Janni meant. Her friend's enigmatic style of painting and illustration had, when she'd first encountered it, surprised her, even shocked her. There had been deeper undertones, too, initially, of betrayal, even fear.

Once, she had given Janni a picture of her black dog from which to produce a portrait, hoping to use the resultant image for the cover of a folder of short stories written by her A-level students. The story chosen as the title piece was about a dog. Fay supposed she had imagined a bland likeness, and was thus lost for words when she came to view the end product – almost a caricature. The texture of the coat was exaggerated almost comically. She had known it would be difficult to portray its dense blackness because of the way the light played upon it, and had wondered how her friend would deal with this. Janni had transposed it into petrel blue, viridian, magenta... it was only later that she came to understand the visual power Janni's creative force really had, and felt ashamed of her own limited comprehension, her desire to see something safe, unchallenging to the eye, raising no questions – subordinate to her own creation. Now, she found herself anticipating with pleasure Janni's inevitable insight into the character of the flowers and wondered what aspect of this moment in the year she herself would undoubtedly have missed, knowing the discovery would be a source of delight.

The two women made their way, one with ease, one with effort, back up to the top of the hill where they had picnicked, taking a last look at the colourful vista below. Then they

A Day for Janni

turned to make the downhill journey back to the car. Walking slightly behind Janni, Fay noticed the appearance of bald patches on her friend's head. *Head-scarf next time?* She averted her eyes quickly. No, probably a full head of hair again, she told herself forcefully. One read about it all the time. The complete recovery, the benchmark passed, all the boxes ticked in the 'right' columns. She had successfully mastered the onset of these strong emotions by the time Janni had leaned across from the driver's seat to unlock the passenger door.

Once inside her little terraced house, Fay sat and listed Janni's dress requirements. In a fortnight's time they would shop and lunch and laugh.

They didn't. Janni telephoned a few days later.

'Fay – *darling* girl!'

'Is everything all right, Janni?'

'The *doctor* rang.'

Fay felt a weight in her chest somewhere that was not the flutter of hope.

'They want me to go back in and have some more surgery. So our shopping may have to wait a bit.'

A week later, a letter arrived, from Janni's sister who explained that the further operation had revealed new tumours. Unconnected, they said, with the original cancer, the abatement of which had initially filled everyone with quite unreasonable hope. She was sending the picture, she wrote, separately. Janni had completed it, and wanted Fay to have it before the bluebells had completely vanished. Fay laid the letter down on the table. She dropped her hands, upturned, into her lap and sat quite still.

The painting arrived the following week, boxed and wrapped in thick, shiny, brown paper. Fay placed it on the shelf near the clock. There would be a right moment to open the wrapper, to look on this, Janni's last gift. For it *was* the last, she knew.

Janni's sister called that evening. Janni had died, peacefully, at two o'clock that afternoon.

The funeral was held in Seaford, attended by a very large number of people. Janni had been loved by many. Fay added her simple knot of violets to the ocean of elaborate floral tributes with a card that read: '*My dearest friend, lost too soon.*'

Returning home, Fay made a pot of tea and took Janni's picture, still wrapped, from its place on the shelf. Taking a pair of nail scissors, she made careful, gentle snips in the parcel tape that secured the edges of the package. When she had satisfied herself that the wrapping was sufficiently loosened not to cause any damage to the contents, she withdrew the small picture and gazed on the work of her lost friend. Oil on canvas: not the conventional medium for pale, wild flowers... but, of course, *these* colours were rich and deep. Fay ran her fingers very, very lightly over the raised oil colour, tracing the line of the stems, the flower-bells. Her tea grew cold.

May blended into June; July arrived – mercilessly hot that year – then August. On her cycle-rides, on walks with her dogs, Fay saw the bright leaves dust over, the grass lengthen and bend, matting the pathways with a yellowing carpet. The end of the year arrived, as it will, celebrations a little dulled without the visits to Janni at Christmas, at New Year. Fay had always been a rather solitary woman. She had acquaintances,

spoke to neighbours, greeted the familiar dog-walking frater-
nity, but had no other close friend. She missed Janni terribly.

Winter stepped aside at length, spring tinting the lawns and
roadsides with mauve, gold and white. Fay walked her hills
and rivers, cycled her woodland tracks and the year seemed
set for entry into summer.

On entering the hall one morning after a long walk by the
river, Fay stopped before Janni's bluebell painting, placed
where it caught the late morning light. Releasing the dogs'
leads, she reached up and took the picture from its hook, gaz-
ing intently at the image. The bells of the flowers had an
almost spiky look. They were not, of course, *blue,* but composed of streaks of red and violet, with stems of sharp
aquamarine. Fay laughed aloud and set the picture on the shelf
above the fireplace, propped up against the clock. She recalled
the day of the picnic: how properly these flowers evoked that
day and the simple exuberance of her dear friend.

Her gaze travelled to the dining room table where, in a
large, water-filled beetroot jar, stood an enormous bunch of
bluebells, past their first freshness, beginning to pale into
white, a fine dusting of their pollen spreading below them on
the glossy mahogany table. There would be no bench for Janni, no lines on brass to proclaim her once delighted presence
on a Kentish hillside in May. Fay would still go there. Resist
the urge to take with her a scanned, colour copy of Janni's
painting and pin it to any and every wooden post where it
could silently proclaim: *Look! The same beauty through different eyes.*

Life as a happy journey – that's how Janni saw it. Fay
wept, then, thinking of how the lives of most people she knew

resembled a relentless quest for emotional and physical comfort. Janni's use of colour was not comfortable, not a search for perfection – just a happy statement, like her life.

Having climbed the stairs wearily, Fay lay down for a moment on her bed upstairs in the small house. Her tears cried out, she needed to deal with the flatness, fill the empty space within. Feel...

Hungry. Sitting up, she swung her legs over the edge of the bed and began to plan lunch. Cream cheese and lettuce; cheddar and pickle; vegetarian pâté with watercress and tomato… She'd make a picnic, enjoy a quiet day out on the hill; a day on which she could celebrate the gift of friendship, be thankful for the time she herself had left on Earth. Long enough, she hoped, to see many more years' bluebells – what colour are they, *really?*

Fay laughed softly: deep within herself she began to experience a slow, rising joy.

Hamish

Is like Eleanor
in these ways:
He is the colour of fire
and quick to flame;
His symmetry and poise are pleasing to the eye
- though *his* shoulders have a military precision;
He invites affection – and yet, if delivered incorrectly,
can take off a finger with his sharp teeth.

He seems, at times, not to need anyone at all.
Yet at other times he will come very close to you
as though to say, Listen, you and I could actually be friends.
And you have to bite your tongue for fear of the words
that will break the truce. But you needn't have, he will wander off
anyway
eventually;
he is a cat that has living to do,
and has no time for those that don't....
Unless, of course, he has some time..

Hoovering the Roof

Where Hamish can leap and turn and invert himself in a yard of
space,
Eleanor can move, and reinvent moves, or move like moves from
the movies.
At one moment, of course, Ginger Rogers,
gliding across the floor – with a slightly perplexed Astaire
wondering, Who the hell is supposed to be leading here?
And the next, a fifties swinging doll, hair sleek and golded in the
disco lights
(even if it's not, and she is alone in her bedroom).
She got funk, she got soul, she got banghra, she got rock and roll;
She is an artist of the dance floor – slightly ahead of the beat
as her brain races on, sculpting new moves for the next bar,
and if she is there first, well, whose fault is that?

Eleanor has to work for a living
and likes to try different roles in the customer service world.
Hamish once wandered in to her shop
as though checking out this extra bit
of his Mirror Girl,
then wandered just as casually out.
Nothing bought, including the lifestyle.
Hamish is a cat of leisure.

Eleanor and Hamish sit at opposite ends of the sofa.
Hamish lies on his own stair – two from the top –
while Eleanor twirls and whirls and makes history in her bedroom.
Amongst the discarded costumes, she winds her way through the
mess – and comes out much improved.
Hamish is by his bowl waiting for food – stiff backed at the indignity of his position.

Hamish

Eleanor is on a bar stool in an unfamiliar bar: short jacket, wide
belt, uncomfortable heels –
stiff backed at the indignity of her position.

Hamish is in Eleanor's bedroom drawer – amongst the underwear
that the rest of us cats can only wonder about. Surely the fifties
chic doesn't end at the shell?
Hamish won't tell Eleanor's secrets: they are siblings – children
of the Red.

Eleanor is having a birthday party. She likes wine and good food
and her friends around her. She is not the girl of everyman's
dreams –
young fools buying the gay man's lollipop template –
but I know, for a fact, that she is the girl of some.
She laughs her laugh, and spins her moves
and someone passes her the wine – and receives a smile well
worth receiving –
She may nip outside for a cigarette…

Hamish rallies his cat army to battle back the fox invasion.
Eleanor loses another hand, and waits for the man who can take
her.
Poets dream Super 8 memories of creatures they have liked:
the moves, the temper, the tempo, the colour of their hair…

the different ways they please him.

Hoovering the Roof

Me, John and a Bomb DEBI ALPER

John Griffiths pushed his bike up the steep slope leading to the platform. His heart hammered against his ribs with an intensity unconnected to physical exertion. He had checked out the station in advance, so he knew what to expect. Indeed, his research had been meticulous and he had reconnoitred every station within a five mile radius before selecting East Dulwich as the one most suited to his purpose.

At the top of the slope he looked up at the dot matrix indicator. The train to London Bridge was due in four minutes. He had known it would be – another result of his research. But any delay – broken down train, leaves on the line, industrial action, or any of the other supposed causes in the pantheon of great railway excuses of our time – had the potential to throw his plan into chaos.

But no. The train was on time. The weather was good – nondescript – a bit dull, but dry and unremarkable. The people on the platform were as he had predicted. Late commuters, most of them. The arse-end of the rush hour. Those who through need or necessity would work ten to six instead of nine to five. Or maybe ten to five with no lunch break. John Griffiths had little idea about the boundaries regulating working in an office. Or working anywhere else for that matter. He'd never had a regular job.

All he knew on that late summer morning was that conditions were ideal. No unforeseen circumstances had intervened to make him change his plan. John Griffiths had been secretly hoping for some such intervention. It was such a good secret he'd kept it from himself too. But when the hoped-for miracle failed to materialise, he saw no alternative but to continue on his chosen path.

At the top of the slope, he turned the corner onto the platform and, swinging his leg over the bike, pushed off on the pedals. He wobbled the length of the platform, keeping his front tyre on the yellow line painted three feet from the edge, marking the danger zone.

Please stand behind the yellow line. Allow other passengers off first. Move along the carriage. Keep your luggage with you at all times. Rules. Warnings. Exhortations. Danger lurks everywhere. Every action implies risk. Every inaction is fraught with potential disaster. Life can change between one breath and the next.

The Angel of Death is hovering over East Dulwich.

Waiting... Waiting...

John Griffiths concentrated all his attention on the yellow stripe like a drunk attempting to walk a straight line. He pedalled to the end, furthest from where the train would appear. Turning back to face down the length of the platform, he placed one foot on the ground for balance. His breathing was ragged, the tautness in his chest preventing the deep breaths that may have eased the tension.

This end of the platform was empty. The seasoned travellers knew the train would come to a halt further down. There was a faint hum as the vibrating tracks heralded the imminent arrival of the 09:35 from Sutton to London Bridge. A buzz of expectation ran along the platform as people stood from the benches and moved forwards, jostling for position to where they calculated the train doors would be, readying themselves for the race to an empty seat.

John Griffiths felt a rising wave of nausea, his stomach knotting high in his chest. His hands, slick with sweat, slipped on the handlebars. Balancing both feet on the ground, he wiped his palms down the sides of his jeans and rolled his shoulders in their sockets. The movement made little impression on the tension in his upper back and neck. His breath strangled in his throat and he suppressed a retch.

The train was coming into view. The mechanical tones of the tannoy announced its destination and warned those on the platform to stand away from the edge. John Griffiths tore his gaze from the approaching engine and swept his eyes along the platform. A young blonde woman rose from the bench nearest him, folding her newspaper and hefting her bag onto her shoulder. She glanced towards him and, for a frozen moment, their eyes locked.

John Griffiths wrenched his gaze away and forced his focus back onto the train approaching platform one. He could see the driver but was determined not to make eye contact. Self-absorbed though he was, he was aware of the effect he was about to have on this unknown man's life. He knew that if he allowed the driver to look into his eyes – into his soul – it would make the part the man was about to play even harder.

John Griffiths wasn't a bad kid. He was uncomfortable with the knowledge that he was about to cause suffering to others.

Swallowing a groan, he pushed off with one foot and pedalled back down the platform towards the approaching train. Head down, focusing not on the train, nor on the tracks – and certainly not on the unsuspecting driver – but on that thin yellow line, he began to pick up speed.

Along the platform, the other commuters fixed their attention on the moving train. No one looked up to see the bike speeding towards the front of the engine. At the last possible second, John Griffiths wrenched the handlebars, turning the bike towards the rails. His hands, drenched with sweat, slipped – but it didn't matter. He didn't look up, so didn't see the horror wash across the driver's face, or the moment when realisation would register on the faces of the waiting passengers. The moment when they would be forced to confront the unanticipated turn their morning was about to take.

All those plans – meetings, interviews, schedules… All those assumptions that had, up until that exact moment seemed so safe to take for granted… All was about to change, sending expectations of the day ahead into chaos.

The bike launched from the edge of the platform, hovering in mid air for one suspended instant. John Griffiths released his sodden grip from the handlebars, reaching out with his arms in crucifixion pose to embrace his fate. The cycle crashed down onto the tracks and disappeared, mangled and twisted, beneath the front of the engine.

The route from Sutton to London Bridge was George Bailey's favourite. The journey took him through leafy suburbia into urban grime and on into the beating heart of the city. On the way, he would see many of the major landmarks –

Tower Bridge, the lopsided glass hive housing the mayor's office, the winking light at the top of Canada Tower...

George had wanted to be a train driver for as long as he could remember. Other kids veered between dreams of becoming astronauts, footballers or fire fighters. But not George. Never mind the shifts, the unsocial hours, the wrangles over safety, pay, conditions... those were petty irritations to be tolerated as the price of genuine fulfilment and job satisfaction.

He passed the green signal and eased the train into East Dulwich station. Some idiot was cycling along the platform towards the train. He had placed himself at the far end – probably unaware the train wouldn't stop that far up. The kid was racing along, his legs pumping the pedals with maniacal intensity. No need. There was plenty of time. The train hadn't even stopped yet. Enough time for Bike Boy to reach the opposite end and cycle back again at the speed he was going.

Something clutched in George's gut. Some premonition. There was something about the way this kid was hurtling along, shoulders hunched, head down.

He was only feet away by the time George registered that his dream job would never be the same again. At the last possible second, the kid twisted his handlebars towards the tracks, head thrown back, his arms stretched out in a triumphant crucifixion pose.

Even as the bike launched in the air, George Bailey knew lives would be changed by that instant. The ripples would spread. The actions of this one unknown kid would have a knock-on effect on the dreams and assumptions of everyone there on that day. And they in turn would bring that changed influence to bear on all who knew them. For each of them, nothing would ever be the same again. Chaos theory in action.

Hoovering the Roof

George saw the bike leave the platform and hover in midair before he screwed his eyes tight shut. He howled in despair.

Joanna Madeley checked her diary. It promised to be one helluva day, starting with a case conference that was going to be a real epic. Joanna was going to have to pull out all the stops to persuade the other professionals that Jade's children shouldn't be taken into care. Then wall-to-wall meetings for the rest of the day.

She rubbed her temples. So much responsibility… so much power… so much depending on her… Sometimes she wondered how long she would be able to carry on. Would she know when she had reached burn-out? Or would she continue to struggle through, not seeing any alternative? Perhaps making mistakes that had the potential to wreck lives…

Joanna popped an indigestion tablet into her mouth and gave herself a mental shake. One day at a time, she thought. Move on auto. Here comes the train… Stand up from the bench… If she was lucky, she'd be able to grab a seat. Use the twelve minutes it would take to get to London Bridge to cast a final eye over Jade's case file…

Gareth Simpson straightened the papers on his lap and put them back in his briefcase. He pulled his mobile from the pocket of his pin stripe suit.

'Gina? Tell Pearson I want to see him in my office. I'll be there in twenty minutes. There's a whole yawning chunk missing from his report. If we don't get it ironed out this morning before the deadline, we'll be out of the running.'

He listened for a moment, aware of the pain building in his temples and knew his blood pressure was galloping up the scale.

'*What?*' he roared, oblivious to the startled looks from those sitting next to him on the bench. 'Well, go and get him *out* of the bloody coffee shop then! Look. My train's just coming in now. Tell Mr Must Have Caffeine that if he's not in my office waiting for me by the time I get there, we're all going to be looking for new jobs, starting with him.'

Jane Radcliffe glanced at her watch. If the train was on time, she would have ten minutes to get from the station to Guy's Hospital. She was running it tight – she hadn't anticipated the delay talking to Gemma's class teacher. Jane pulled the envelope from her bag and, extracting the letter from the Oncology Department, stared at the few lines again, even though she knew them by heart. Why did they call it *Oncology*? Why not *Cancer*? Or just plain *Death*?

Jane knew from the statistics that many women survived nowadays, but that hadn't been the experience in her family. Her mother and two of her aunts had died of breast cancer. She had watched each of them journey from diagnosis to surgery, to radio, to chemo. And she had watched each of them wither and die. Icy fingers clutched at her guts. How would Phil cope? What about the children?

The tracks began to vibrate. The train was on time. In a few minutes, she would be sitting opposite the consultant and would hear what her future had in store for her.

Martin Saunders adjusted the volume on his iPod. The line of coke he'd snorted before coming out was beginning to wear off. He could feel the confidence and bravura that he needed to get through the interview seeping out of his pores.

He checked the dot matrix indicator. The train was due. Taking a last drag from his cigarette, he ground it out beneath his heel. He was early. There would be enough time to duck into the toilets and do another line before the interview.

Tom Dickard – a name that produced sniggers swiftly replaced by respect and fear in those he met – checked his schedule. His mobile chirruped an unlikely version of the Sugar Plum Fairy. Tom listened as his business partner told him the change of plan. The first visit was to be the one originally listed as third on the list. The Hodgson family. The woman had got herself a job and would be leaving home at 10.30. They'd have to push it to get to Whitechapel before she left. Mary Hodgson would be looking forward to another day working at the café. The arrival of Tom and Bill would soon put paid to that. By the time her husband and kids came home, they would find their living room bereft of tv, dvd player and stereo.

Tom grinned. It was great being a bailiff. He derived genuine pleasure from being the agent of other people's misfortune and had nothing but contempt for people who took on debts they couldn't afford. They deserved whatever they got.

'OK, Bill,' he grunted into the mobile. 'The train's coming in now. I'll be there in twelve minutes, then we can go and kick some arse.'

Blossom Adoke folded her copy of the Metro and sighed as she watched the train approach. Another day. Another boring day. Seven hours of moving figures around spreadsheets before she would be on the opposite platform on her way home again. Just marking time. If only something different – something unpredictable – would happen.

Me, John and a Bomb

Suky Higham had always hated her name. She had been conceived, born and raised in a succession of children's homes. Her mother, Sue, and her father, Kieran, aged fourteen and fifteen respectively, had been unable to care for themselves, let alone a baby. Though they had thought differently at the time.

They were in love – or believed they were – neither having personal experience of the condition. They had dreams of living together as a family – a flat or maybe even a little house. Home, anyway. A real home. The powers that be thought otherwise. Suky was passed from children's home to foster parent and back to the home again in a pattern that repeated itself over the years until Sue and Kieran finally succumbed to the inevitable, Kieran disappearing into the underbelly of society reserved for the unloved and damaged before his daughter was out of nappies.

When Suky turned seven, she saw her mother for the last time. Sue visited her daughter on her birthday at the foster home where she had lived for the previous six months. Sue took in the flash people carrier in the driveway, the spacious rooms, the lavish furnishings... The foster parents seemed kind. There was even talk of Suky being adopted into the family. I could never give her anything like this, Sue thought. She'd be better off without me...

She gave her daughter the colouring book and crayons she had bought, compared them to the expensive gifts she'd received from her new family, and made her decision. Sue kissed and cuddled her child for the last time, told her to be a good girl – and disappeared.

Hoovering the Roof

A week later, an envelope slid through the letterbox and onto the parquet floor. Seeing her name on the outside, Suky ripped it open and read her mother's plans. *It's for the best,* the letter said. *Don't try to contact me. I love you.*

Love? the seven-year old Suky thought. What kind of love was this? What was it about her that made her parents *love* her, but never want to see her again? Enraged, rejected and confused, Suky declared war.

The foster parents weren't bad people. No one can say they didn't try. But the tantrums, the constant confrontations tipping into acts of violence and destruction, the sheer hatred they saw blazing from Suky's eyes, eventually wore them down. The final straw came when she tried – with some success – to set fire to the living room curtains (hand woven Indian silk). Suky landed back in the children's home.

At fourteen – the same age her mother had been when Suky was conceived – she dropped the vowel from her name and insisted on being called Sky. Practicing her signature aged fifteen, it seemed logical to dispense with the 'am' in her surname. Suky Higham evolved into Sky High. At sixteen, her final attempt to run away was successful. There was no one left to care enough to put in the effort that would be needed to find her.

Sky High became a statistic, a non-person. She had no National Insurance number, no credit cards or bank account, no official documentation of any kind. She didn't exist. All she had going for her was a resilience born of desperation and a determination to survive at any cost. Her prime motivation was to wreak revenge on all those who had let her down. Which was everyone.

Against all the odds, she managed to avoid the twin pitfalls of hard drugs and prostitution to which so many girls in her position succumbed. Her vision of bringing down the society which had created her was what kept her strong and focused.

She kipped on floors and in squats and occasionally on the streets, keeping her eye on her wider vision at all times. Not just surviving, but surviving for a purpose. Chipping away at the system using the skills she had learned. Theft, fraud, arson, sabotage. The traditional tools of anarchy. She spent hours in libraries, reading her way through the politics section, finding a context for her struggle. She knew she had a part to play in history, even if she was currently acting alone. Her life had meaning, direction and purpose. And she was diligent in its pursuit.

The train was approaching the station. Sky folded her newspaper and hoisted her bag onto her shoulder. As she glanced along the platform, she noticed a young guy on a bike staring at her. He looked away, but not before she had clocked the intensity in his eyes. Even at this distance she could see the sweat beading his brow. She watched as he pushed off and pedalled towards her, keeping his front wheel on the yellow line on the platform edge.

Sky frowned. She had her day all planned out – a familiar agenda based round the stolen cheque book and card in her bag. She needed to stay focused and forgettable. Especially forgettable. When she was on a mission, her main aim was to blend in to the point of invisibility. It was why she stayed at the top end of the platform away from the other commuters. This guy was moving into her space. As she eased forward towards the train, she could see him from the corner of her eye. What was he up to, cycling so fast along the edge of the platform?

95

Hoovering the Roof

Schooled in the actions of the desperate, Sky sussed John's plan at the same instant as the train driver. At the last possible moment, mere feet from her left hand, John Griffiths wrenched the handlebars of the bike and launched himself into the path of the oncoming train, his arms outstretched in classic martyr pose.

Sky High had no time to think. She reacted from instinct. In the millisecond that the bike hung in the air at the peak of its flight before plunging into descent, Sky reached out. Grabbing the about-to-be dead guy by the back of his denim jacket, she pulled backwards with all her strength.

John Griffiths couldn't believe it. He was still alive! How could this be? His meticulous plan had failed at the last moment. Instead of oblivion, he still had all his senses. He could see the sky, taste his fear. As the train's brakes stopped squealing, he could hear a bird singing in the bushes in the sudden silence and smell the buddleia blooming behind the fence.

And he could feel the platform hard under his sore body – except not quite.

He pushed himself up on his hands, realising his fall had been broken not by some*thing* but by some*one*. The young blonde woman he had noticed earlier squirmed sideways from under him. Before John could work out what had happened, she swung her right arm and punched him on the shoulder. Hard.

'Shit!' she exploded. 'What the fuck did you want to go and do that for?'

John Griffiths goggled at the woman, rubbing his shoulder. The impact of hitting the platform had winded him. The knowledge that he was still alive had shaken him to the core.

Me, John and a Bomb

But there was more to add to his confusion. He stared at the woman's hairline. Her blonde bob had slipped sideways, revealing a shaved scalp covered with dark stubble. And she looked very angry.

As his mind struggled to take in this unwished-for slice of life he had been granted, he heard nervous giggles and realised they came from him. Following his line of vision, the woman reached up and yanked the wig straight.

'C'mon,' she grumbled, struggling to her feet. 'We've got to get out of here.'

Only then did John Griffiths become aware of the ashen-faced train driver stumbling from his cab and the open-jawed stares from the people nearest to them on the platform. The train doors hadn't opened and the irritated passengers on the train and those waiting to embark were preoccupied by the interruption to their schedule, most of them unaware of its cause.

'Come *on*,' the woman urged, pulling at his sleeve. 'You've already ruined my fucking day. Don't make it any worse. Fucking leg it, will you?'

Still unable to comprehend this unexpected turn of events, John Griffiths stumbled to his feet and did as he was told. Together, the unlikely pair charged along the platform, barging aside anyone too slow to get out of their way.

This is the first chapter of the fourth book in the Nirvana series of thrillers set in South East London. The first two, **Nirvana Bites** *and* **Trading Tatiana***, have been published by Weidenfeld & Nicolson and are available online and at good bookshops.*

Hoovering the Roof

Carmex HELEN HARDY

'You just can't say stuff like that!' I say as we leave the party.

Lorelei gets in the car and winds down her window. I've given up telling her it's more fuel efficient to use the air conditioning. She says she likes to feel the breeze on her face. We aren't moving yet, but she stares out anyway, turning her face away from me, into the warm night. I'm distracted by the way the red lights from the car ahead of ours glint off her curls. All the other women hereabouts straighten their hair for special occasions, but not Lorelei. Then I remember the conversation and my frustration bubbles up again.

'I mean,' I go on, almost imploring, 'like saying that Sarah lost her sight in a freak shaving accident – what's that about? When you talk that way, people just think you're lying, or crazy. Half our neighbours think you're nuts...' I tail off. I wonder where I'm going with this, and feel slightly ashamed. Lorelei tends to have this effect on me.

'It's true,' she says, and I know that she's not agreeing with me, she's talking about what she said inside. I open my mouth, but I can't think of anything more to add. We're still not moving, someone's stuck up ahead, their wagon too wide for turning in the narrow part of the driveway. Lorelei turns to me at last, pouting a little without realising it, and I have to lean across and kiss her. She isn't wearing lipstick, just balm – Carmex, out of the little yellow pot. The taste takes me right back.

I was fourteen, walking along the road with Doug. Both of us were kicking up the dust as we went, in a way calculated to ruin our shoes if they weren't already battered half to pieces. We slowed down outside the store, out of habit. Neither of us had any money that day, but we looked in the window anyway, at the fading candy bar boxes. That was when something flew out of the door of Frank's bar up ahead and crashed to the ground, sending up a spray of dust better than anything our feet had managed. The object rolled towards us. There was something awkward about the movement, and I realised that it wasn't round after all, it had eight sides, and a large bump on one surface. It wobbled over onto the flat base and stopped, right at our feet.

'What is it?' Doug wondered. He kicked it, gently at first and then a little harder. The object was about a foot wide and black under all the dust, with a rough-looking texture like lizard skin. Each of the corners was re-enforced with an extra piece, held on by brass studs. There were smart brass clips tethering three alternate sides, with a set of hinges on the fourth.

'It's made a bit like a coffin,' I hazarded, thinking about the brass handles and fittings when they buried grandpa.

'For what?' Doug scoffed, but he stopped kicking the box.

Carmex

We both stared at it some more. No doubt we would have opened the thing eventually, but we had to bear in mind the way it had hurtled out of the bar. Presumably its owner remained inside and might emerge at any time.

'Remember that picture of an octopus?' Doug said. 'The one on the wall at school? A small one of those'd fit in it just right!'

We were so wrapped in contemplation that we didn't notice the girl until her hi-tops came within the orbit of the black box. Her shoes were even dirtier than mine, but you could tell they had once been lilac, and the legs that emerged from them were long, skinny and, in my eyes, perfect.

'I'm Lorelei,' said the girl, 'and that there is my daddy's hatbox, the one that holds his 4-inch brim.' We gaped at her. 'My daddy's a cowboy,' she explained. She sounded proud. 'We should leave,' she added. 'Like, now. He's gonna be real mad with whoever threw that out here, but he won't thank us when he comes after it, either.'

Doug looked freaked, and said something about his dinner. He ran off home, and Lorelei and I went to hide round the back of the store, where she kissed me. To this day I have no idea why. And don't think it's like we've been together ever since – her father moved on somewhere after the fight, I guess, and I never saw her again until last year, although I recognised her right away.

I'd never felt or tasted anything like her lips. They sent a warmth right down my spine, besides the more obvious places. I licked my own lips, afterwards, to get the aftertaste of her balm, that sweet butterscotch richness set off by an undertone of something medicinal, almost antiseptic, that I've thought of all my later life as the taste of innocence.

'It's true!' Lorelei repeats, as I release her.

'It doesn't matter,' I say, but she's all set to explain.

'Sarah was very short sighted anyway, you see. She was shaving her armpit in the shower and she had her face right up close to see what she was doing, and her hand slipped. I mean, I don't really know what happened exactly, it was a safety razor I guess, but still…She only lost the sight in one eye, but it was her good eye, so now she's almost blind.'

I'm thinking about how Lorelei knows stuff like that, how people tell her things, but I guess I just look blank.

'It sounded better the way I told it inside, right?' Lorelei insists. 'Sometimes, explaining too much just ruins a perfectly good story.'

The driveway ahead of us is clear at last.

'Right,' I say, and drive on.

Baby Crabs ANAND NAIR

Asha watched the wet tarmac unroll in front of her like a luminescent ribbon of grey as the car sped past the little shops and coffee haunts that beaded the national highway. The wind lifted the stray bits of her unruly hair and the earthy smell of new rain brought with it memories of other rides along this road. This had been her father's favourite road: the short stretch that led from the little town of Thalassery to the Dharmadam seaside.

'No watching little crabs in the sand-holes this time.'

A thin edge of panic threaded the commonplace remark she made to her father's presence in her head. Walking the beaches of Dharmadam, only a morning's walk away from her home, searching for little crabs and shells had been a frequent Sunday morning pastime of father and daughter. And afterwards they would eat a hot breakfast of *dosha*, at one of the wayside stalls. The flat white crêpes would be sizzling hot, straight from the stainless steel griddle, served on pieces of banana leaf. The tang of the fresh ground coconut chutney served with it would stay with them while they trudged home on damp feet covered in soft, wet sand.

Hoovering the Roof

Her panic now was symptomatic of all the sudden changes in her young life, which a quiet, predictable and carefree existence with her widower father had not prepared her for. Sometimes she felt that her father had abandoned her by dying when she had been away at College in distant Bangalore.

This young man who had been chosen for her lived in busy London and was hardly likely to know about the holes in the wet sand that looked like bubbling porridge when the waves frothed at the edges and withdrew. From these holes the baby crabs crept out and scurried around playing hide-and-seek, swiftly disappearing from one hole into another.

She stole a look sideways at her brand new, just un-wrapped, fiancé. Well-worn Levis, she registered, and a black T-shirt that had *'London Marathon, 2003'* written in three-inch-high white letters on it. Cheap Casio watch on the wrist, sun-bleached strands of brown wrist hairs escaping from under the black watchstrap. Brown leather chappals that had seen a fair bit of wear. Black hair, cropped short, and a faint whiff of sandalwood soap windward, elusive like the strains of a long-lost melody.

Asha felt a little overdressed in her new churidar-kameez outfit, a concession to her clucking Aunt Seetha. There were times when you gave up on the small tussles to concentrate on the big battles. And living with Aunt Seetha was like being in a straitjacket padded with love and attention, mostly surplus to need.

'Get out of bed now, it is past six.' 'Bathe and get dressed.' 'Comb your hair and put some oil in it to keep it down.' The instructions were numerous and well meant. But Asha could do with being left alone a little – or even a lot. In her father's house they had gone about their day in their own relaxed way, meeting up as and when; the instructions had been few and far between.

Asha looked sideways again at her companion for the day. He has a way of being quiet, almost switching off, in crowds, she thought – as he did when he came to her house for the 'pennukanal' ceremony, accompanied by mother, elder sisters and uncles, all eager to inspect and put in their two-penny-worth as to whether or not Asha was good wife material for Mithran. He must have liked what he saw, because the marriage broker was back only two days later, saying that the family would like the marriage to go ahead, if Asha agreed. She hoped that he would not do his quiet act all day today; was he as nervous as she felt?

As if in answer to her unspoken thought he turned round and smiled.

'Hope you didn't mind my hijacking you like this today.' No contrition in his voice, she noticed. 'I put up quite a fight to get your aunt and uncle to agree to let you out for the day.'

'It is kind of you to take me out.'

Asha was polite, non-committal. So much was decided for her by her family of aunts and uncles recently that she had learned to pick her battles with care; going out for a day with Mithran was the least of her problems.

Today, right now, she wanted her father desperately to tell her what to do, faced with such a major change in her life. She wanted him to say what he thought of this young man. Did he approve?

'I thought you'd like to know a bit more about me – and I need to know what kind of a person you are.' Mithran broke into her reverie, sounding tentative.

The car glided and bumped along, trying to negotiate a difficult battle with the potholes that alerted her to the fact that he had turned off the highway, onto a side road that led to the Taj Seaview Hotel. Mithran, at the wheel appeared to be concentrating on the roads, the dead pie dogs to avoid, the State Transport buses hurtling down murderously towards them. Asha watched the uniformed, cow-licked, school children, walking four abreast, on their way to one of Kerala's innumerable schools; she felt she had been one of those laughing children a few months ago.

Mithran could not have been aware of the dialogue going on in Asha's head, but he may have sensed that she was uneasy and a little wary. How should this first encounter begin, between a newly engaged couple who knew zilch about each other, except caste, age, looks, family background and educational level, missing out all the important bits, like how much they registered on the honesty, loyalty, compassion and such like measures.

Asha knew from her aunt that Mithran had agreed to an arranged marriage, though he had reservations about the whole process, because he wanted to please his ageing parents. And after six years working in London, apparently, he really had not met anyone he was desperate to spend his life with. But he insisted he needed to know that this young woman had not been coerced into marrying him, that she was a willing participant.

It was a very reluctant Aunt Seetha who had, after many misgivings, allowed Mithran to take Asha out for the day, unchaperoned. Mithran had insisted, showing a stubborn side to what seemed his usual pliant personality.

'We are engaged. We are getting married in a month and we don't know each other at all. That is how it is done here and I will go along with that. But we need to talk and not with fifteen relatives buzzing around within hearing distance.'

Mithran's sister, who had conveyed the demand, was quite clearly embarrassed.

So the family had reluctantly agreed, quite apprehensive about whether Mithran knowing Asha better would be a very good idea, before the young man was firmly hooked, tied and delivered. The whole idea was to get Asha married *before* Mithran found out what a handful she was.

She had turned down quite a few eligible men on what looked like mere impulse. And then Mithran's family had turned up, trailing behind the broker, with matching horoscopes and no dowry demanded. The aunts and uncles held their breath on the '*pennukanal*' day. Asha refused to dress up for the event with something that sounded dangerously like, 'He can see me as I am'.

Surprisingly, some chemistry must have sparked at sight. It could even have been the quiet courtesy of Mithran after all the look-her-up and-down furtively and stroke-the-moustache antics of some of the would-be's.

But Asha had said 'yes' and nobody was asking whether the reason was desperation to get out of her claustrophobic existence with her aunt and uncle, since her father died. Or really because she saw something in that moustache-less computer man from London that no one else could see.

And he was only going to take her a fifteen-minute drive away to Dharmadam, Seetha had reassured herself. Asha had not had a conventional Kerala upbringing with her widowed father. In Seetha's opinion, the girl had got a lot of silly notions about independence and equality with men in her head. And going off to Bangalore to do that course in Media Studies had not helped either. She had come back even more stroppy and unconvinced that she should appear submissive to her future in-laws, if she ever wanted to get married. In fact, it had been quite a struggle, getting her to wear a half-decent looking outfit, let alone a sari, and a pair of gold earrings, on this outing. She was determined to look as ordinary as possible.

'That rust *salwar-kameez* set does make you look stunning,' Aunt Seetha had admitted as she left. 'But that hair…'

Now, with the breeze in the car, 'that hair' was showing a mind of its own. Every time she pushed the strands off her face and tucked them behind her ears, they came back with a vengeance. It was like sweeping ants into a dustpan.

'Your hair…' Mithran started.

'…is unmanageable,' Asha finished for him, a mite defensively.

'Actually, what I was going to say was, a lot of women in the UK spend a great deal of time and money trying to get that casual look, which you are fighting with.'

Asha did not know whether to take him seriously. Was he having her on? A pixie grin lit up his face and made him look like a provocative schoolboy.

Asha was into unfamiliar territory here; she was not used to compliments about her hair. All her life people had told her that it was not long enough, it was too curly, there was too much of it, she did not know how to manage it ... But she did stop tugging at her hair.

Before she knew what to make of his banter, the car was sweeping into the drive of the Taj hotel. The commissar with his red-and-gold plumage was opening the car door obsequiously, and the in-house driver was taking the car away for parking.

Baby Crabs

Asha gingerly climbed the mirror-smooth pink granite steps; they seemed especially designed for the unwary to slip on. She thanked the Lord that she was not wearing the high heels that Seetha had tried to coax her into. As if she did not have enough to negotiate!

The lobby, all chrome and plate glass, was large enough for a tennis court. She noticed that unlike the men she was used to in Kerala, Mithran did not stride ahead masterfully, while she gathered *duppatta* and handbag to follow a good ten paces behind. He opened doors for her and stayed close, eventually helping her to settle down at one of the window tables that looked on to the veranda on the west, and the steps leading to the seaside. The muted roar of the sea was a familiar and unobtrusive background to the subdued murmur of guests relaxing on the veranda.

Drinks turned up as if on cue, and it occurred to Asha that Mithran seemed familiar with the place. He relaxed into his seat.

'I want to take you down to the water when you've had that drink, and show you something, it's only a five minute walk along the beach. I often come here when I am on holiday in India.'

'That will be really nice. I was hoping we could take a walk down that way. But it is really at its best early in the morning.'

Mithran looked surprised that she had been to the hotel before. A little bit beyond the beat of a small-town girl, he must have thought. The surprise showed.

It was Asha's turn to grin. 'You are quite right; I have not been inside here. But my father and I used to come to the beach on morning walks. You can get to the beach from the little path that runs down from the other side of the hotel en-

109

closure. And you can get lovely food and hot, real coffee, on that path, if you know where to look.'

'There you go,' said the voice in her head. 'Might even find some crabs if the sun is not too high.'

They sauntered down to the waterside, Asha, still hanging on to her lime juice. 'Us small town girls are not used to ice-cold drinks, you see. So we cannot get them down in a hurry.' She was teasing him and he looked as though he was beginning to enjoy the company of this more vivacious Asha.

Mithran sauntered towards the boundary fence, which separated the hotel beach from the hoi-polloi on the other side.

'See that flat rock over there?' Mithran pointed to a rock surface, which glinted, in the near distance, breaking surface on the water only when the waves retreated. 'You can pick mussels from there. And in the sand...'

'...the little crab babies run from one hole to another, playing hide-and-seek.' There was a sliver of sadness in her tone.

Mithran picked up her arm and tucked it into his. His touch was as light as the gentle sea breeze flicking her curls. 'We shall come here whenever we come on holiday and walk down your path. We could pick mussels and see the crabs.' Clearly, he had guessed the sorrow in her voice earlier was for the memory of her father; his family would have told him that they had been very close.

'And eat *dosha* and coconut chutney at the stalls.' Asha's smile was a happy one.

'You like him too, don't you?' Asha asked her father. But she did not wait for an answer. She walked on, curling her fingers on his arm, holding on while she looked expertly in the sand for baby crabs

110

Thrust Out MARK ARRAM

Thrust out   poetic bleakness
Gets us going   but you still a bit sad
Bonjour tristesse   born again
Sunglasses on   headscarf on
We walk   wet in our pants

Delivering authority   standing for justice
One boy crying   pain
Soon another one   this time shame
No nonsense   no bullying
Fist in the back   *get inside*
Nasty preacher's son   God don't stop him

Shell BECCA LEATHLEAN

At eight p.m., Mrs Jones jumped up from her chair.

''Night,' she said, as she scuttled towards the bedroom.

After a few minutes, her seven-year old daughter, Ciara, followed her. Her mum was in bed, curled up tight with the sheets pulled up around her chin. Ciara could see she was still wearing all her clothes, and under the covers she could see the outline of her mum's sensible shoes.

Ciara went back into the living room. The coal fire was going out and it was cold. She watched TV for a bit, but she couldn't concentrate so she fetched her pyjamas and sat in front of the fire to change. Then she closed the vents on the grate and placed the guard in front. It was too cold to clean her teeth so she went straight to bed, sliding in between the icy nylon sheets.

Ciara tried hard, but she just couldn't sleep. She had a hollow, frightened feeling in her tummy. It was freezing. The piles of toys – soft toys, hard toys, even her big metal dolls' house on the bed, shifted on top of her as she moved. When the hands on her bedside clock said nine o'clock she sat up.

113

This wasn't right, was it? she thought. She needed someone to talk to. She needed a hug. Her mum couldn't help, but
she couldn't risk being heard. So she got up and went over to
the window.

Ciara unhooked the arms and pushed the window right out.
Then she clambered up so she was lying across the length of
the frame and swung her left leg over. The notches on the
frame dug into her tummy while her foot hunted for the ledge
near the ground outside. Then, holding on tight, she swung
her right leg over and slithered down. She was outside in the
dark. Bare feet on icy pink gravel that glittered in the pale
moonlight.

Ciara walked over to the wire fence that divided their drive
from Hilary and Roy's next door. She pulled up the wire,
ducked underneath and walked up the side of the house to Hilary and Roy's back door. Heart in her mouth, she gave a
timid knock.

Hilary opened the door. 'Ciara! What are you doing here?'
she asked.

'I couldn't sleep,' Ciara said.

'Where's your mummy?'

'She's in bed. She's got one of her "moods".'

Ciara liked Hilary and Roy. They were ever so friendly.
Glamorous, too. They were always really kind. But Hilary
was frowning.

'Your mummy will be so worried if she wakes up and finds
you gone,' she said.

Ciara felt a lump rising in her throat, a panicky feeling in
her chest. But then Roy came to the door.

'Ciara!' he exclaimed. 'What's wrong?'

Shell

'Ciara's a bit upset,' Hilary said. She turned to face Roy, and said something so quietly that Ciara couldn't hear. The couple looked at each other for a moment. Then Hilary turned back. 'Come on in,' she said, gently. 'Come and sit with us for a while.'

Ciara followed Hilary and Roy through the kitchen to the comfy sitting room. The lights were low – she'd never been there in the evening before. She started to relax. They must like me after all, she thought.

Roy smiled kindly. 'Make yourself at home, young lady,' he said, and Hilary asked if she'd like some Ovaltine. Ciara didn't know what Ovaltine was, but Hilary said she'd make it in a special mug – and she said it would help her to sleep.

While Hilary was making the Ovaltine, Roy asked Ciara if she'd like to see their tropical fish. By the wall there was a big aquarium and, swimming inside, lots of big, bright sea creatures. There was a triangular fish with yellow stripes and some little tiny fish in shimmering tones of blue and green. Lurking at the bottom there was a big brown crab with eyes on top of its head and massive black pincers. It was looking right at Ciara. She had never seen anything like it.

Roy told her the names of all the different fish – Angelfish, African Chichlids, Damselfish and Golden Whiteclouds. It was like a magic world.

Ciara stared back at the crab. It didn't move, so she tapped on the glass. To her surprise, the crab disappeared. Its head vanished into its shell, clamped tight shut.

'She won't come out again now,' said Roy.

All of a sudden, Ciara felt very sad. But then Hilary came back from the kitchen with the Ovaltine. She sat on the leather sofa and patted the spot next to her, inviting Ciara to sit down.

Hoovering the Roof

Ciara sank into the squishy white leather and Hilary put her arm around her. The three of them talked about fish and the taste of Ovaltine. Ciara wasn't sure whether she liked it – it wasn't as nice as cocoa. And it was so late! Half past nine! She'd never been up that late before.

When she finished her Ovaltine, Ciara said she was feeling better and she'd go home now. Hilary and Roy came to the back door and watched her out.

When she was back on her side of the drive, Ciara hooked her fingers under the window frame and pulled it out. She put her head and shoulders underneath. Feeling the weight of the glass against her back, she climbed up on the ledge. Lying flat and holding on tight, she swung a leg over and pivoted for a few seconds before pulling the other leg across and sliding to the floor. Then, relieved she had made it, she got back under the nylon sheets.

Her mum was still in bed across the hall, and soon Ciara fell asleep. Her head was full of all she'd seen next door: the soft white sofa, the pretty fish swimming round and round in their tranquil night-time world – and the mysterious crab with its staring eyes, tucked up tightly in its shell.

The Black Madonna of Derby JOANNA CZECHOWSKA

Pan Nowak started on his usual lecture. Standing beneath the image of the Black Madonna, slit-eyed, golden-brown, hanging on the wall, he began.

'No other country has suffered so much and achieved so little as Poland. We were partitioned between our greedy neighbours and disappeared from the map of Europe for centuries. Polish children were beaten for speaking their native language – Marek! Sit back on your chair right now – we came from under the Russian imperialist yoke after the First World War and became a free nation again. But only for less than 20 years. Then we endured the Nazi invasion and the Germans and Soviets again carved up our country between them. How could the British celebrate Victory in Europe when the whole point of the war was lost, freedom for Poland? When will we ever be free?'

Pan Nowak had tears in his eyes as his speech reached a crescendo, while the children in his Saturday morning Polish class continued to chat, fight or flick bits of paper to each other.

Hoovering the Roof

Wanda Baran sat looking out of the window. A grey pall hung over the wet streets of Derby, yet even they seemed more welcoming than sitting in an upstairs room of the Polish Club among the stale smells of bigos and cigarettes. At 14, she felt large and out of place in a classroom surrounded by much younger children. The teacher, Pan Nowak, was now discussing various grammatical declensions and relating them to some obscure Polish poet. Wanda drew a little heart on her exercise book, she picked some old nail varnish off her thumb and then rested her head on her arms. She had to go to school every other day so why, when all her friends were out in town shopping and meeting in cafés, did she have to go to another school on Saturdays? Zosia sat behind her, constantly putting her hand up to answer questions and diligently learning the stupid poem off by heart.

'Why do they always live in the past?' Wanda thought as she drew a flower on her exercise book. The future was the only thing that mattered to her. She didn't care about these old people, old wars, old quarrels. It was history that caused wars – if people didn't know about the past, they wouldn't fight over it.

Wanda didn't care about the past because there was some-thing in her immediate future that interested her so much more. That very afternoon, Wanda and her two best friends, Pam Haines and Susan Browne, were going to the ABC cine-ma in Victoria Street to see a film that had just come to Derby, *A Hard Day's Night*. And the thought of that film was the only thing that was keeping her going all through this bor-ing, boring lesson.

When Pan Nowak finally dismissed the class, Wanda grabbed her books, raced downstairs, out of the Polish Club and down the street. She left Zosia talking to the teacher and helping him tidy up the class. Zosia would have to bring Janek home, she thought.

She knew there was just time to get back, have something to eat, put on her make-up, new top and skirt, then run out to meet Pam and Sue outside the cinema.

It was a twenty-minute walk back home to 16 Porton Crescent. This semi-detached house in a quiet residential street full of quiet residential neighbours had been the Baran family home since 1961; a definite step up in the world, another rung on the social ladder. Wanda ran up the front drive and let herself in with her latchkey.

'Hello,' she called but wasn't surprised there was no reply. Her father was probably still working as Saturdays were one of his busiest for painting and decorating. Helena was food shopping and Babcia was, no doubt, having a lie down.

Up in her bedroom, Wanda changed quickly, then bent towards the mirror to apply her make-up. She hated her nose, long and punctuated by a series of bumps and dips. It cast a shadow over her face, reminding her of a sundial. Her lips were very, very thin, her eyes were brown like her father's, her hair was blonde and one ear was rather cauliflower shaped. She was short and she was tubby. Her large hips crushed into her new green denim skirt, her bosom wobbled in her tie-dye red top and she pulled on creamy yellow half-length boots. She had painted her chewed fingernails red and applied green eye shadow to her eyelids. After considering her reflection, Wanda grabbed an old headscarf and draped it over the mirror to obscure the image entirely. 'That's better,' she murmured then rushed out of the room and slammed the door.

Zosia and Janek were entering the house as Wanda was leaving.

'What are you all dressed up for?' asked Zosia.

'I'm going to the flicks with Pam and Sue.'

'So what are you all dressed up for? Oh, didn't you realise – the cinema only works one way. You can see them but they can't see you.'

'Sod off,' retorted Wanda.

'Excellent argument,' yelled Zosia as her sister ran down the drive, 'you should have been a lawyer. Anyway, those colours don't match – you look like a traffic light.'

'Traffic light, traffic light,' taunted Janek.

As Wanda ran towards the bus stop she looked down and saw her sister was right. Never mind, too late to change now, the bus was coming. Wanda got off at Victoria Street, and saw Pam and Sue waiting for her outside the cinema. She noticed they'd managed to steal a few cigarettes from their parents and were practicing lighting up. She saw them look at her and say something to each other. They were probably commenting on her clothes and make-up. She suspected they laughed at her behind her back but today, Wanda really didn't care.

'Hiya, kids,' she shouted happily. 'Are we ready to rock and roll?'

Pam and Sue were both dressed in knee-length boots, short sleeveless dresses and their hair was tied up with chiffon headscarves. They played around with their cigarettes, feeling adult and sophisticated. Wanda realised it helped Pam and Sue's confidence to hang around with her and she knew the boys' glances quickly passed over her and on to them. But friends, any friends, were a vital part of social success.

Anyway, she knew today all rivalries would be forgotten. Today, all three of them were excited – they giggled, bought popcorn, and checked their make-up in little pocket mirrors. Girls packed the cinema – the noise and feeling of excitement were stiff in the air. The girls found their seats and spent the next two hours bouncing up and down, chewing their handkerchiefs and screaming at the top of their voices. They could hardly hear a word of the film.

When Wanda came out of the cinema, everything was different, she felt different, the world was different. The shops, cafés, even the pavement and lamp posts in Victoria Street were lovely, the world glowed – she was in love. She bought the LP, a huge poster and a T-shirt. She went home, put the record on her small box record player, hung the poster on her side of the bedroom wall and lay on her bed. She buried her face in her pillow, hugged it in her arms and sobbed, 'Paul, Paul'.

She wrote him letter after letter. And received a black and white photograph from the fan club with his signature across it. Zosia said it was just a facsimile and they printed millions of them for idiots like her, but Wanda knew he had actually signed it and she pressed the photo to her bosom and kissed the image's lips with her own thin lips. Eventually the picture became rather soggy, the edges dog-eared, and there was a deep crease in the corner.

But the photo provided her with some comfort when news came that Zosia had passed the 11+ exam and would be going up to Pinecrest Grammar School for Girls. There was much family celebration and Barbara smiled with obvious delight.

'You're just like I was at your age,' she soothed. 'Beauty and brains – a winning combination.'

Tadek patted Wanda's hand comfortingly.

'Don't worry, sweetheart. I don't mind that you didn't pass it. You're still my number one girl.'

'Well we have a lot in common, don't we? We're both thick and fat and ugly and failures, aren't we?' And Wanda ran from the room, slamming the door.

This chapter comes near the beginning of the novel **The Black Madonna of Derby**. *The year is 1964 and Wanda, the eldest daughter, is asserting her independence from her Polish parents and their cultural identity. This is in contrast to her younger sister, Zosia, who yearns to conform to those edicts, particularly as instilled in her by her beloved but matriarchal grandmother. Which will be strongest – the new society or the old customs?*

Heroes FERDI MEHMET

This cold cuts through the hardest men.
The ruthless reminder – the sun shall expose us again.
The darkness that cloaks our Soul is ripped away by
 the Dawn,
Mocking,
Reducing Might and Glory to distant Dreams.
Where are they? Those that stood Tall,
Climbing to Victory,
With only Passion,
Strength,
Unity?
Did our spirit flee from this Light?
And the poetry of the Robin,
The smell of Glory,
And the taste of fresh new dairy?
Neighbours greet and wish us Paradise.
Her enthusiasm is repulsive,
From a universe of Joy and Ecstasy.
We too danced to that melody.
And our neighbour dreamt of eggs and coffee.
The Battle was won, the possibilities infinite.
A Thief crept in and stole our Prize.

Hoovering the Roof

Our game was weak, yesterday's news.
The Agony, the Remorse.
Oh, the Shame.
The Looking Glass portrays Hideous Reflections of the heart.
But wait…
To Crumble in the jaws of Adversity never drove us
to Overwhelming Heights.
The Haven holds a Secret.
We remain Faithful, search and strive,
For the Gift that lies in All Places,
For the Gold we held so close, so tight.
And we shall Clutch it once more,
Today!
No time for Breakfast, for Fuel,
No time for expired Symphonies,
The orchestra lunges Heroes into gear,
Relentless,
Unforgiving.
Prepare.
The Day grows Bright.
And so shall we,
Higher than ever before.
A simple leap of Faith, or more,
For that which is Alien?
Authentic Soul.
No Trickery, away with the Promise of War.
This Day we Present Heart.
Lord, how We Triumph.

Wearing the Tread KATHLEEN HINWOOD

Dirt sprayed up through the spokes as the bike pitched forward. Tommy leapt to safety.

'Hey, what did you do that for?'

Miriam stood up. Tommy remained silent next to his bike. His mouth hung loose, gormless.

'Hey, Frog, look what you did.'

She scraped mud off the rug and threw it in the air. Tommy shuffled forward. He stood between Miriam and the bike, unable to come closer. His boots were leaden. His face soured with something far more pressing than guilt over childish antics. Miriam relented; no harm had been done.

'So, what's your name, kid?'

He told her, simple and soft. Patting the rug, she beckoned him over. Tommy slunk forward, slipping down beside her.

'What's going on, Tommy?'

'Nothing much, I guess.'

Typical response. Miriam didn't have much patience with kids but she needed practice. Jack had a son about the same age. She wondered where the hell Jack was and then exhaled.

Patience. Perseverance.

'That's a good looking bike you've got yourself.'

He shrugged. Miriam had her work cut out for her. She hoped Jack's kid would be easier to handle. Where the hell was Jack, she wondered.

'Why don't you eat something, Tommy? I've got plenty of food here.'

He nodded. Miriam piled food on to a plate and handed it to him.

'Why did you call me Frog, before?'

A little voiced peeped from the silence. Thank God.

'Well, you looked a bit like one. Your mouth was wide open and I'm sure in this weather you'd probably catch a fly.'

He smiled. Progress. Small. It was fleeting but something had shifted.

'I'm Miriam.'

He didn't respond. He ate.

'Where do you live, Tommy? Is it far from here?'

Again, nothing more than a negating gesture. He chewed on a drumstick.

She thought of his parents. She knew he wouldn't say any more than he already had. A little boy in the park on his own and his name was Tommy. Short mousy hair, too young for the burden he held. He had a new bicycle; it was blue and silver, abandoned on the path. Wasted on the ground. Filing a police report in her mind, she observed Tommy more closely. Was blue his favourite colour? Was it his bike or someone else's? Uncertain, as Miriam had only seen him swiftly in flight. Should she reprimand him or be his friend?

'Let's get your bike off the path.'

Miriam patted his knee. He flinched.

'Don't you want it?'

'I don't care.' Then, he started to cry. Silent tears. Miriam felt uncomfortable. She got up and retrieved the bike, bringing it over to Tommy.

'It looks expensive. We wouldn't want to get it stolen. I don't think that would make your parents very happy.'

'I guess so.'

Fuck, this was hard. Her problems, submerged under the weight of his anxiety.

'I got it today. It's my birthday. Now, it's ruined like everything else.'

'Hey, Frog, it's my birthday too. My friend was meant to meet me but he got caught up with something.'

Jack always got caught up with something but she didn't want bitterness. She smiled. Keep it light.

'Frog, you're alone on your birthday too.'

She couldn't elicit a response as he rolled himself into a ball. Miriam was ensnared. She admired Jack's tenacity with Rob. He was a good dad. Fuck. This is all bullshit, she thought. Resolute, she focused on drawing the boy out of his shell.

'OK, Tommy.' She patted him on the back. 'Hey, little Frog, talk to me. Have some chocolate. Do something. Tell me something'

Panic rose. She thought of Jack and Rob. A little trust, a little quiet, peace. Subsiding panic. She came close to Tommy and wrapped her arms around him.

'Tell me your secret.' Tommy's shoulders eased but Miriam kept a firm grip.

'It's all my fault.' Such petulant childlike exaggeration, but Miriam knew that Tommy's problem was big.

'Hey, Frog, speak!'

'I killed him, I killed him, I killed him,' he wailed.

'I'm sure it wasn't like that.'

Miriam felt certain that such a little boy couldn't hurt anyone. Tommy's head hung low, his shoulders oscillated in rhythm with his breath. She didn't want him to be broken. Miriam eased her embrace.

'Tommy, I think you need to tell me what happened. I'm sure it's not your fault.' His guilt was real, shifting, wanting to take blame.

'I could have saved him.'

'Saved who?

'My brother, but I let him die.'

Miriam felt the shift, pleased that he was no longer calling himself a killer.

'It was my birthday. There was a bang. Simon was inside. I was outside playing. I didn't look straight away. I heard the bang but I kept on playing.'

Miriam listened as he revealed his burden, strangers with a secret.

'When I looked back to the house, it was on fire. I could see Simon through the flames but I didn't do anything. I couldn't move. I didn't know what to do.'

Tommy's voice cleared. The heat consumed Simon. Miriam could see him melting away.

Fire dissipates, but the embers remain. Tommy talked. His words were circular. Every now and then, Miriam interrupted. His voice had steadied. A lightness began to infuse Tommy's language. An abscess had burst and Miriam swabbed it clean. He climbed into her lap and squeezed her as their secret evaporated. Tommy slid out of the embrace on to his feet. Strangers, once again. He picked up his bike that lay on the rug, and sped away, as only a child does.

Miriam waved to him. She lay down on the rug, closing her eyes against the sun, enjoying the solitude, the respite. She rested, contented.

****

A light breeze washed over. A childish murmur emanated through the trees. Miriam woke, expecting to see Tommy return but it was Rob hurtling towards her.

Now she knew what to do.

Hoovering the Roof

Deathless RICHARD WOODHOUSE

'He described how voices sometimes whispered and sometimes screamed at him. He was asked what the voices told him to do, and he said they threatened to kill him. He was asked why they should do that. He replied 'shadows, you know it's the shadows you know, and it's... at the door threatening...'
From Court of Appeal Judgement on the Stockwell Strangler Kenneth Erskine, R v [2009] EWCA Crim 1425 (14 July 2009)

Jack had only been in the country a few hours and already he could feel the vultures circling around him. He needed somewhere to think – perhaps the hidden apartment? No, the brick, concrete and steel of London's buildings were oppressive after the African plains. He needed space. Even though he was nearly home, he made a short detour to Brockwell Park. Pulling the car over, he stepped out, stretched his spine and walked up to the fence. A night bus roared by: in the cones of its lights he saw that the gap he usually used for entry had been mended. Without missing a step, Jack sprang over the iron spikes and leapt into the park.

When his eyes adjusted to the gloom, he saw brooding trees silhouetted against a stained orange sky. Beneath his feet was a vast grey carpet of grass. About him lay piles of metal barriers, dumped in preparation for the Lambeth Country Show.

Though he felt knackered, his mind was buzzing. Snapping into a run, he ascended the hill. Jogging through darkness didn't frighten him; he was far too canny for that. The heat and heady scent of midsummer enveloped him. By the time he reached the top of the hill he was sweating hard. He liked to feel his body work – it calmed him.

Jack slumped into his favourite wooden shelter. He often exorcised his troubles here. Surveying the city he called home was always a pleasure. Its lights sparkled across the valley like diamonds tossed across black velvet. From up here it was hard to imagine the noise, the grime, the energy.

'*How many people have died down there, do you suppose?*' said a wispy voice.

Catching a glimpse of a man beside the shelter, Jack turned. But when his eyes came to rest on the place, no one was there. His sweat ran cold.

'*Over the centuries, I mean,*' the voice continued, '*how many have died in that captivating city?*'

Jack looked every which way, but saw no one. 'Where are you?'

'*Come now, are you not the least curious? How many?*' the voice insisted.

Jack turned to the lights below.

'I... I don't know, millions I guess.'

'*How many of them chose to remain, do you suppose?*'

'I don't know what you're talking about. Leave me alone.' Leaping up, Jack circled the shed.

'You are troubled.'

'That's because I'm talking to you.'

'You know of what I mean.'

Jack humoured the voice, expecting to unearth its source any moment. 'Oh yes, my life's a mess, is that what you mean? I can't even end an old relationship.' Jack put his hands over his ears.

'Why can you not?'

The voice was as loud as ever.

'Christ, what am I doing? Leave me alone!'

Jack strode off down the hill, but the voice pursued him.

'Why is it so hard?'

'Because we've been through too much together.'

'So why leave her at all?'

'Because it's only a matter of time before my wife finds out, and she deserves better.'

'Does she?'

'Yes, damn you, she does. She's under terrible strain. My affair with Molly could break her.'

'If you truly value her life you had best leave London.'

Panting and dripping with sweat, Jack came to an abrupt halt.

'What are you talking about?'

He span around and around seeking the source of the disembodied voice.

'And you should leave tonight.'

'Why? Who are you? What do you know?'

'Too much,' said the voice in such a melancholic tone Jack felt sure it was no boast.

Head in hands, Jack dropped to his knees. 'I'm tired. Leave me alone. Leave me alone.'

'Heed me, Jack. I came to warn you. Mistakes have been made. You must protect...'

'FUCK OFF!' Jack rasped.

After that, all he heard was the gasping of his own breath and the pumping of his own heart. He was oblivious to the soil beneath his knees, which would always support him – until the day it consumed him.

The house was as silent as a pressed flower.

Dawn lay huddled into a ball still unable to sleep – the letters in the lounge troubled her. Where was Jack?

She heard a scream.

Elsa was having a nightmare – again. Dawn dragged herself out of bed, slipped her slippers on and crossed the landing to her daughter's bedroom.

'Are you okay, honey?'

She stroked the damp blonde hair off her forehead. Elsa clung to her and whimpered. Dawn comforted her. By and by, the little girl returned to an innocent's sleep. With a kiss, Dawn pulled herself away.

Walking past the study, she noticed the computer was still on. She frowned, certain she had switched it off. Where was her head these days? With a sigh and a shake of her head she shut it down.

Dawn left the study, intending to return to bed, but at the head of the stairs she hesitated. Then, vacant-eyed, descended.

Ignoring the letters in the lounge, she pit-patted across the hall's chequered tiles and entered the kitchen. She turned on the kettle. As it coughed into life, she opened the fridge and fanned her nightdress, letting the cool air waft around her hot body.

The letters continued to prey on her mind. Resisting the impulse to read them, Dawn placed a camomile tea bag into a cup. The kettle clicked and sighed. She stared at the boiling water as it doused the tea bag.

Voices in her head repeated, '*Go on, go on, go on.*'

She replaced the kettle and left the room.

On the kitchen counter the camomile tea steamed, forgotten.

She crept into the lounge, switched on a table lamp and opened an alcove cupboard. Kneeling, she removed a black shoebox and placed it on her bare knees. Hands shaking, she lifted the lid on her stalker's mind.

You would think being shot in the head would be the end of most people's troubles, but Jack Nave is not so lucky. Trapped in a vegetative state, he begins a journey of self-discovery and finds there is more to life than death. Who killed him and why? These should be the sole concerns of his wife, D.I. Dawn Moore, but there are darker things on her mind – such as her stalker and Jack's secretive past.

The novel **Deathless** *is available from lulu.com*

Hoovering the Roof

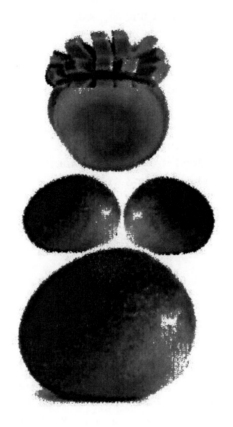

Mango BECCA LEATHLEAN

I was out shopping the other day. It was cold and grey, and I'd slogged my way to the market with a heavy heart. The bus was packed as ever – I was wedged into a mass of cold, un-yielding South London bodies and the air was thick with tuts and sighs, toothsucking and general disgruntlement, until it tipped us all out in front of Brixton tube.

So there I was, walking down Granville Arcade, past the fruit and veg, the African snails, the yam and plantain and green bananas, and all at once I was reading a sign above a pile of nice, fresh juicy fruits that said:

Lady, lady, please don't squeeze up, squeeze up me mango!

I felt myself shrinking, softly. It was not an unpleasant feeling – as I got smaller I got warmer, sinking comfortably into myself. My innermost core started to glow, the warmth spreading into my skin.

137

As I shrank, the London angst began to melt away. I could feel my bones relaxing and my skin smoothing out – oils starting to trickle throughout my system. All the sour feelings were turning deliciously sweet. Drip by drip, a feeling of warm contentment percolated through.

I wrapped my arms around myself, hugging in all those good, rich feelings, and I felt my legs being sucked up – my bottom grew larger and firmer to accommodate them. I could feel my bottom starting to glow! My heart was pumping; a steady, rhythmic beat. I could feel my blood circulating – it was turning into sweet and juicy liquid. I was so juicy, I could have burst, except for the firm skin holding me in. I felt fluid but secure and supremely confident sitting up there under the stallholder's cheeky sign. I was glowing like tropical sunshine on that cold, dark London day.

A Greater Gift RACHAEL DUNLOP

Grandpa always said that he liked working with used cars because they had stories to tell. New cars, they were bores, just talked about themselves, they knew nothing else to talk about. Used cars, though, they would talk to him and he would know who to sell them to. Which I found hard to believe, to be honest. Everyone knows used cars are really cagey.

'Grandpa,' I once asked him, 'how do you know they are telling you the truth?'

'Well,' he said, 'why would they lie?'

'Oh, you know, if they'd been stolen or their clock had been turned back, or the chassis number switched, that sort of thing.'

'But I could easily check that out. That's why your salesman is usually the one lying, not the car. They don't care what price you sell them for. No, I meant, why would they lie about the other stuff?'

'Other stuff?' I had no idea what he was talking about. I didn't know what Grandpa had always known, since the day he got his Gift, that a good car was more than the sum of its parts and service logs. He fixed me with his gaze for a moment, long enough for me to think that he could hear *me* thinking.

'If you don't know, son,' he said at last, 'it's not for me to tell you. Maybe you'll know, one day, if you've got the Gift. If not, well, it's none of your beeswax. I might want to sell you a car some day.'

He smiled, but I could see this was deadly serious to him.

Not many people saw Grandpa in a serious mood. As a used car salesman in a small town, he said he always needed to be 'on', like a performer. Trust was his most valuable asset. 'Even when I'm not in the showroom,' he said, 'when I'm just in the store or coming out of church or walking the dog, I'm still Doug Clark, Used Car Salesman. That's what people think when they see me. I'll never just be Doug Clark again until I stop selling cars.'

Grandma said this was why Grandpa was always so tired at the end of the day. It was only when he closed his own front door that he could relax. Except Grandpa never came through the front door: he liked to come down the side of the house and in through the kitchen door, with its glass panels already steamed up from whatever Grandma was cooking for dinner. I was usually at the kitchen table at this time of day, trying to cram my homework in before we ate. I never got started on it earlier: Grandma always insisted that I go play outside as soon as I came home from school, rain or shine.

'You need to make some space in your head,' she said. 'Keep an empty corner free for whatever might come.'

For some reason, she felt plenty of fresh air would help the process.

Grandpa would come sit at the table still in his coat, just sit, quietly, for ten minutes or more. When I first came to live with them, I thought maybe he was sitting down to talk with me, that this was 'our' time. But Grandma soon put me right.

140

'He feels a responsibility to those cars,' she would say with a little shake of her head. 'Some of the things they tell him, you wouldn't believe. It's a burden. And, you know what cars are like, they know what they want. And they tell your Grandpa, all day long. He needs some time just to quieten his head.'

I didn't know what cars were like, and neither did Grandma for that matter, as neither of us could talk to cars. We had to take Grandpa's word for it. There weren't many people who could talk to cars then, and I often thought it was a Gift that should have paid more, just for its scarcity value. Grandpa laughed when I told him that.

'I suppose I could move up to some fancy dealership,' he said, 'but rich people don't buy used cars, they only want new ones. And the new ones don't know who they want to belong to. They hardly know themselves yet. No, I'll stick with the used ones. Them I can help.'

I liked to go to the showroom with Grandpa on Saturday mornings and help out. The lot was on a wide road near the edge of town, catching the traffic in and out from the west, and the cars were lined up against a high chain link fence that butted up to the road. First job on a Saturday was to wash the cars: in the summer they sported a fine layer of greasy dust; in winter they were smeared with the white crust left behind by the hard frost. I watched Grandpa as he moved around the cars, trying to see how he did it, see if there was a trick or technique. Not all Gifts are hereditary of course, but I hoped this one was.

Grandpa worked his way around the lot, holding a one-sided conversation with the vehicles. At least it seemed one-sided to me. Grandpa said the cars didn't really talk to him in words, it was more images and sounds and feelings. But even though they didn't think in words, they understood his words well enough.

After my parents died, some people thought it strange that Grandpa stayed in the car business. To people in general he would say: 'I have the boy to support now. I need my business more than ever.'

To me he said: 'It wasn't the car's fault. It never is. A hit-and-run like that, it's the person driving that's to blame.'

One Saturday morning, Grandpa and I were sitting in the showroom when Mrs Banks came in. Grandpa shooed me out.

'Go make some coffee,' he said, 'You know how I like it.'

Mrs Banks was notoriously shy – people stared at her feet, hovering as they did three inches off the floor.

'She finds it hard,' Grandma told me, 'having a Gift everyone can see all the time, and not even a very useful one. Says it makes people think she's somehow frivolous, floating around like that.'

So Grandpa sent me out back while he served quiet Mrs Banks. Anyway, I liked that he finally trusted me to make the coffee right.

I flipped out the basket and filled the paper filter with coffee grounds. *Not enough,* my head said to me. It was like thinking with someone else's voice. I shook my head as if to shake off a persistent fly. I slid the basket back into the coffee maker. *Not enough,* my head said again. I pulled the basket back out, added a shake more coffee. *Yes.* It was like having a party line in my head. There were my own thoughts and then these others, separate, parallel.

Oh great, I thought, Grandpa gets the Gift of talking to cars and I get kitchen appliances? I stuck my head around the door into the showroom. Grandpa and Mrs Banks were out in the lot, looking at a small car. Grandpa would look at the car then talk to Mrs Banks, then look back at the car again. I brought a fresh mug of coffee out to the desk for Grandpa and sat in his swivel chair, turning myself to and fro as far as the cubicle would let me.

That hurts, my head said.

I slowed the swivel down and listened. Nothing.

'Huh,' said Grandpa from behind me.

'What?' I said, spinning around to face him.

That hurts.

I grabbed the edge of the desk, stopping the chair mid-spin. Grandpa was giving me that look again. After a long moment he reached around me and lifted his coffee.

'Oh, nothing,' he said. 'I think Mrs Banks is going to take that little Honda.'

'That's good,' I said.

'Hmm.' Grandpa sucked on the hot coffee. 'You can go along now,' he said, 'I've got things covered here.' As I was heading out of the showroom he called after me: 'Good cup of coffee.'

The next Saturday, Grandpa left me behind when he went to the showroom.

'It's a nice day,' he said on his way out the door, 'Go out on your bicycle, play some ball with your friends.'

I lowered my head over my pancakes and didn't reply. Grandma snapped off her rubber gloves and came to sit beside me.

'You could do worse than work on your Gift today.'

'How did you know?' I asked.

But Grandma always knew. It was a gift, although not a Gift. Grandma didn't have a Gift.

'Do you want to tell me about it?' she asked.

So I told her about the coffee machine and the chair, and the myriad other mechanical devices that had insinuated themselves into my head over the past week.

Grandma pulled a pack of unfiltered cigarettes out of her apron pocket and lit one up, tapping the ash into her cupped hand as we talked.

'Best keep quiet about this one,' she said. 'People will give you no peace, wanting you to fix their toasters and their blenders and what have you.'

'But I could do that,' I said, 'I mean, for a living. Grandpa uses his Gift for his job, right? I should do the same.'

Grandma shook her head. 'I know they tell you in school that if you get a Gift, you have a responsibility to nurture it. That if it's a useful Gift, well, you've got to use it. You get the Gift that's right for you, they say.' I nodded. 'But the way I see it,' Grandma continued, 'it's all pretty random. Gift or no Gift, you've got the right to do what makes you happy. Do you want to be a repair man?' I hadn't really thought about it. 'Just keep your options open,' she said.

After a few weeks I stopped asking Grandpa if he wanted me to come to the showroom with him. He never said no, but he was full of suggestions for what he said were better ways I could spend my Saturday mornings. He didn't fool me. I knew what he was up to, why he didn't want me near those cars.

I told Grandma I would work on my Gift on the weekends, but secretly, like she said. Sometimes I went to the library to look up the Gift Guides. Other times I just walked around town, trying to work out what Gifts people had, or how they used them. Some I already knew about – like old Sammy Partridge who had spent the last sixty years starting fires with a flick of his thumb and who had never been allowed within ten feet of a gas station. Or Theo Stebbins, who could sort of slide away until you just didn't notice him anymore, even though he was standing right in front of you. The ones that had their Gifts in their heads, like me, they were harder to spot.

After an hour or so, I would make my way over to the showroom. On the far side of the road from the showroom was a small ridge covered with stubby grass and sporting an advertising hoarding. I would park myself in the shade of the hoarding, hoping that Grandpa couldn't see me.

Every Saturday, I sat and I watched. I couldn't hear how he talked to the cars, but I could see it. As I got better at tuning into my own Gift, I began to see that some of Grandpa's tricks were the same as mine. People without Gifts imagine some sort of laying-on of hands, but it's not like that. When you are really listening, when it's something important, you need that air between you. Somehow it amplifies the signal.

When a new car came in, Grandpa would spend a good ten or fifteen minutes standing in front of it, hands clasped behind his back. Then he would put a hand ever so briefly on the hood, and, usually, give a small sigh. From my vantage point on the hill I could see it: the outstretched hand, the slight fall of the shoulders. Then Grandpa would move on.

The day it happened was the first real day of spring: a soft day when the air that touched my skin neither cooled it nor warmed it. I had persuaded a vending machine downtown to give me a cold soda for free. I cracked open the can now and took that first slug, too fizzy, too fast, so good. I had been coming to watch Grandpa for months now. It never occurred to me that I might be waiting in vain: I trusted that Grandpa knew what he was doing.

Hoovering the Roof

I had seen the car come in the previous week, upended on the back of a tow truck. Sometimes Grandpa took in cars as a trade, but he bought them in too. This must be one of those. Now it was at the back of the lot, washed and waxed but with no price sticker on it. Which was odd.

Grandpa walked over to the fence at the front of the lot and waved to me. Startled, I jumped up, soda spilling from the up-turned can. Grandpa waved again, beckoning me over. I slid down the hill and crossed the road. Grandpa met me at the gate, laid a hand on my shoulder. He didn't ask for any explanation, and neither did I. He simply said:

'Can you do it?'

'I don't know,' I replied. 'I've haven't been able to talk to cars yet. I've been sort of building up to it. Have you found it?'

Grandpa nodded. 'I've been asking and asking these past two years, since your parents died. Every car that came through this lot, I've asked. I knew it was a long shot, but I think I've found it.'

'You think? You don't know? Haven't you asked it?'

Grandpa turned me around to face him. 'You have a greater Gift than me. You hear it in words. You have to be the one to ask.'

So I followed Grandpa to the back of the lot and I stood in front of the price-less car. And I asked it:

Are you the car that killed my parents?

146

Cascade Mountains MARTI MIRKIN

It's hard to believe there are

    Places like this –

    Still –

    Now.

Hoovering the Roof

When I was little

   I heard the songs –

The Mighty Columbia,

The Columbia River, Blue Columbia

   Rolling on,

   Powering the West,

Giving hope.

An hour out of Portland, Oregon

   And into The Cascades

   first time

   And oh, they bowled me over –

Up the cliffs from The Columbia

   And into paradise.

Cascade Mountains

An odd climate, Oregon,

Pacific Northwest

And so, a vegetation like no other –

As in music, a half beat different.

And waterfalls,

    Many waterfalls,

    I love waterfalls…

Small ones, big ones, double ones,

    Fat and thin, short and long.

Look – here's a picture of

You and me and your friend Lonnie

    In front of a long stream

    Roiling down a mountain

    In multiple cascades.

Lonnie's better now,

Hoovering the Roof

Boyfriend tried to rob her,

Boyfriend tried to kill her,

Shot her through the cheek

And left her for dead –

So

We came to the Cascades to

   Walk her grief with her,

Watch the flow of the Columbia

   Mighty, As a notch in the belt of things moving on

   Churning currents, endlessly changing.

And we watched and we talked

And we ate and we walked

Cascade Mountains

And we came to

   A place from the past –

A simple spa –

A sulphur spring,

A cladded cabin,

Changing room, towels, a skylight,

A room full of bathtubs,

   enamel, clawfooted, old fashioned…

You slowly sink into your own hot bath,

   sulphurous, embracing, steamy –

Up from the core of the earth –

Up from the risen rock deep beneath the Cascades…

Hoovering the Roof

And me,

I breathe in, drink the water, and

Think about the people

Down all the years

  Had the faith,

  Saved the knowledge to

Keep this sanctuary running on

And – here it is today

When we need it.

Dinner with the Colemans FERDI MEHMET

'Fathers should neither be seen nor heard. That is the only proper basis for family life.'

-Oscar Wilde

Melvin and Harriet stood waiting at the door of the Coleman house. Melvin held a bag with two bottles of wine – one red and one white. He was nervous, but eager to meet Harriet's family.

'You'll be fine, darling,' she said, noticing him sweating.

The door opened, and there was Harriet's mum, Caroline Coleman.

'Hey, hello. Come in, come in,' she said, looking thrilled. 'Hi, you must be Melvin.'

'Yes, hi. Nice to meet you.'

The house was warm, and welcoming.

Caroline leaned in close to Harriet's ear and lowered her voice. 'Bit of a change of plan, Harriet. Your dad's business trip was cancelled, so... he's having dinner with us.'

'Oh.' Harriet looked at Melvin, then back at her mum. 'Oh, well… That's okay. Right?'

Caroline nodded reassuringly, but not convincingly. 'Come through, we'll have a drink before dinner. Simon and Rose are on their way.'

Simon and Rose were Harriet's younger brother and sister who shared a flat together. Melvin was yet to meet Rose, but he'd met Simon for the first time earlier that day. They'd hit it off immediately. Simon was only twenty-two, and was floor manager at a restaurant called Montana White's, where Melvin and Harriet had gone for lunch.

Melvin couldn't help but admire Simon. He was charming and confident, with the air and experience of a man many years his senior. He had a way about him – a projection that said he was a man of the world. He made his role in the restaurant look easy, giving orders to staff and greeting customers. He was composed – *pleased* to be working, it seemed. That was rare these days.

Upon seating Melvin and Harriet at their table, Simon had looked at Melvin, tilting his head and curling his lips. It was the kind of expression a mother gave her newborn baby.

'Oh Harriet, he's *adorable*,' said Simon. 'Well done you.'

Then Simon strutted off to the bar for their wine, in his refined grey suit – tailor-made – that he wore with style and grace.

'Nice guy,' said Melvin to Harriet. 'I can tell he's your brother.'

Harriet grinned. 'I hope you're looking forward to dinner tonight.'

Melvin and Harriet sat together at the dinner table. At the head of the table, next to Caroline, was Harriet's father, Randolph Coleman.

Randolph sat with the manner of a king – with *majesty*, his presence filling the entire room. He was unmoved by the company he was in, and he didn't smile. He didn't have to – this was *his* home, and *his* dinner table. His position as the high lord of the manor was perfectly clear.

Everybody was drinking red wine in large glasses.

'So,' said Randolph. '*Melvin.*' Randolph looked hateful, and already unconvinced by anything Melvin might say. 'What do you... *do* with yourself?'

Melvin swallowed the lump in his throat. 'Actually, I write stories. For children. Children's books.'

'Is that so?' Randolph became more focused on Melvin. 'And how *is* that?'

Harriet and Caroline smiled softly at each other.

'I love it,' said Melvin. 'It's great to see kids happy. I mean we all enjoyed stories when we were kids, didn't we?' His smile was too much, too forced – he could feel it.

Harriet looked at Melvin, nodding. 'That's true. I love stories.'

'Oh, *sure*, sure, of *course*,' said Randolph. 'Who doesn't? But writing for small people...'

'For children,' said Harriet.

'Yes, for... for *children*. Isn't that a bit... *lazy*? You know, writing stories for the more mature audience, that's... well, that's more of a challenge, isn't it?'

'Not necessarily, Dad.'

'Kids are quite smart,' said Melvin, trying to sound casual.

155

'And they can be harsh critics. You know, the stories have to keep them interested.'

Randolph held up his wine glass, sizing it up. 'But surely with children you can write any old drivel about, I don't know, flying tigers, and trips through space, or anything of the sort, can't you? Kids eat that stuff up, don't they?'

Melvin nodded. 'True. But the same goes for adult fiction. People making up stories, that's all it is. And kids... they *need* stories. So... you know.'

Randolph watched Melvin for a moment. 'Indeed. Well, it's good to know I could always fall back on children's stories if I ever tried to be a writer.'

'So, Mum...' Harriet's intervention was long overdue. 'When are Simon and Rose getting here?'

The doorbell rang.

'That'll be them now,' said Caroline, getting up to answer the door.

Melvin sat still, not saying a word. So did Randolph, and Harriet. Nobody looked at anybody. Randolph took a sip of his wine, and Melvin did the same. The silence was painful.

'You'll love Mum's cooking, Melvin,' said Harriet.

'Someone's got to,' said Randolph.

The room went quiet again as Harriet's recovery tactic was struck down and washed away by her father.

'Look who it *is*.' Simon was bursting with joy to see Melvin.

'Hey, Simon.' Melvin stood up and shook his hand.

'This is my sister, Rose.'

'Hi, Rose.'

Rose was younger than Simon – about nineteen maybe.

'Hey, Dad,' said Simon. 'I thought you were away. It's nice to see you.'

Randolph nodded. The eye contact he made with his son was quick, almost unnoticeable.

Rose said nothing.

'Well, this is just lovely,' said Caroline, standing over everyone. 'I'll just check on dinner.'

'This lasagne is delicious, Caroline.'

'Thank you, Melvin, I'm glad you like it.'

Simon smiled and nodded. 'Yes, Mum. Delicious as always.'

'So, Rose,' said Melvin. 'Living with your brother now. How's that working out?'

Melvin felt the mood drop.

'It's cool,' said Rose. 'I like it.'

She smiled at Simon, and he patted her on the back.

'It's not like Nazi Germany, which is great,' she said.

'Not like when you lived *here*, you mean,' said Randolph, a vein pulsing on the side of his head. 'If it was that bad, why do you keep coming back?'

'To see Mum,' Rose said innocently.

Melvin looked at Harriet apologetically. She gently shook her head.

Dessert was Caroline's homemade apple pie, with ice cream.

'I agree, Melvin, whole-heartedly,' said Simon. 'Oscar Wilde, he had some great philosophies.'

'He was a smart man,' said Melvin.

'He was a *homo*,' said Randolph. He said it insouciantly, through a mouth full of apple pie. 'Truman Capote, another homo.'

Melvin noticed Simon's face change. He looked uncomfortable.

'Well, they were great men,' said Melvin, knowing this was risky. 'Great minds that left a major impact on the world. There's no denying the importance of their work, you know.'

Harriet was smiling at Melvin, with her hand rested on his knee. Rose seemed detached from the scene, and Caroline looked ecstatic, like everything was perfect.

'They were men who fornicated with other men,' said Randolph.

'In their personal lives, maybe,' said Melvin. 'Doesn't matter. Their writing is exceptional.'

Randolph leaned toward Melvin. He was almost smiling, probably admiring Melvin's guts to delve into this discussion with him. 'How do you trust a man who commits buggery, on another man, at that? It's one of the basic rules of the Bible. "Thou shalt not suck another man's penis".' Randolph sat back, laughing to himself. 'It's unnatural.'

Melvin did have more of a case, but decided to let it rest. He didn't want to offend Harriet's father, and certainly not in his own home.

The sound of Simon's silver spoon hitting his bowl startled everyone. 'Has a woman ever sucked you off, Dad?'

'Hey,' Randolph pointed at him. 'Watch your fucking mouth.'

Rose laughed, and so did Caroline, but hers was an uneasy laughter. Harriet put her hand across her eyes and looked down at her lap.

'Because oral sex of any kind,' said Simon, 'is technically unnatural, a perversion. We don't need it to reproduce but we all do it, gay and straight. And you there, talking about the

Bible. What about "Love thy Neighbour"? You hate pretty much everybody.'

Simon pushed his chair back and stood up. 'There are dozens more hypocrisies surrounding your illegitimate references to the Bible, Father, but I won't go into it. After all, what do I know? I'm just a homo.'

Simon headed for the door.

'Calm down,' said Randolph, not quite concerned. 'I never said *you* were a homo.'

Simon stopped and looked down at his feet. After a second he turned to his father, and said, 'But I am a homo, dad. You know this. I am a homo.'

Simon left the room.

'Thanks for a lovely evening, everybody,' he called.

They heard the sound of the front door gently closing. There was silence at the table. Randolph raised his eyebrows and shook his head. Rose was grinning, trying to contain the hysterical laughter that itched to burst out of her. Caroline nodded and smiled, seemingly oblivious to what just happened. Harriet was staring at her bowl now, mildly smiling – unsurprised after the inevitable finally occurred.

'This is *really* great apple pie, Caroline,' said Melvin. 'You must tell me your secret.'

Caroline winked at him. What was that?

'I liked your story about the wizard who drives a magic bus,' said Rose. '*The Secret Spell-Maker*'. Her gaze drifted away as she smiled, in reminiscence. 'It was… magical.'

'Thanks,' said Melvin.

Rose shook her head and snapped back into reality. 'I'm going for a cigarette,' she said.

Melvin turned to Harriet. 'Um, is it okay if I use the toilet?'

Melvin called his friend Jerry from the bathroom.

'Jerry, this is a disaster.'

'What's happened?' said Jerry.

'What's happened? I'll tell you what's happened. The father's a queer-hater; the brother, who, I should probably mention, is gay, didn't take kindly to his dad's fascist views on the world, and got up and walked out, and I think it's all my fault. And I think the mum was coming on to me.'

'Okay, Melvin, just – wait, what?'

'I think the mum was coming on to me,' said Melvin.

'Oh, shit. Is she... sexy?'

'What?'

'Is she sexy?' said Jerry.

'Well, she's... what difference does that make?' Melvin rubbed his forehead. He was sweating heavily. 'She's... alright, I suppose.'

'Get in there then,' said Jerry.

'Fuck sake, Jerry, I don't want to get in there, she's Harriet's mum.'

Melvin caught sight of himself in the bathroom mirror. He was a mess.

'Well, what did you call me for?' said Jerry.

Melvin looked around the bathroom. 'Actually, I don't know,' he said. 'I don't know why I called you. Okay then, fuck off. I'll see you Friday.'

Melvin pocketed his phone and started running the taps. He splashed his face with water, then patted it dry with one of the towels. There was no real reason for him to panic, but that was Melvin all over. He looked in the mirror, pointed at himself, opened his mouth to say something reassuring, changed his mind, and opened the door to leave.

And there, standing in the hallway, was Caroline. She looked at Melvin, her eyes more fiery than before. She was excited, breathing fast, her lips almost puckered up. She ran a finger down her cleavage.

'Caroline.' Melvin's attempt at sounding normal was pathetic.

'Call me... Mrs Coleman,' she said.

Melvin's heart raced.

'I've seen the way you look at me, Melvin. I know what you want.'

'Oh,' said Melvin. 'I can assure you, Mrs, er, Caroline... Coleman, um, I... I don't know what you mean.'

'Oh, stop it, you. We're alone now. You can tear into me with everything you've got.' She edged nearer and brushed her breasts against his chest. 'I can take it,' she said.

Melvin tried to relax. 'This isn't appropriate, Mrs Caroline... Um, Caroline. Really, we should get back before they send a search party after us.'

'Tear my knickers off,' she said, gritting her teeth. 'Do it with force, I challenge you to be as nasty as you can, boy.'

A door slammed somewhere. It startled Melvin, which startled Caroline. Melvin took the opportunity – he quickly squeezed past her, and darted to the top of the stairs. He saw Rose re-entering the dining room below.

Melvin risked a look back at Caroline. She hadn't moved. She was watching him with narrowed eyes, like the game was on – she was the cat, and he was the mouse.

'Are you okay, Melvin?' said Harriet, as he sat down. 'You're sweating horribly.'

'Yes, Melvin,' said Caroline. She strolled into the room – cool, composed, experienced at this game of hers. 'Whatever is the matter?'

Strangely, Melvin admired Caroline's cunning, and her ruthlessness in her pursuit. Clearly she enjoyed danger.

'Nothing, I'm fine,' said Melvin. 'Rose, could I have one of your cigarettes?'

'You don't smoke,' said Harriet.

'I do now,' he said. 'Ah, what I mean is I kind of fancy one right now. And I want some fresh air.'

Harriet nodded. 'You want some fresh air, so you're going outside to smoke a cigarette.'

'Yes,' he laughed. 'Where's that cigarette, Rose? And a light.'

Melvin was calm after a few moments outside. The sweating stopped, and Caroline wasn't such a threat. What a nymph. Maybe she was bored. Or maybe she was just, quite simply, a sex-maniac.

Melvin began to weigh the pros and cons of telling Harriet about her mother, when the door swung open, and there was Rose. She had a cigarette in her mouth.

'My light?'

'Here.' He cupped the edge of her cigarette and lit as she puffed to get a burn going.

She inhaled, and blew the smoke in his face. He handed her lighter back.

'You want to know my story?' she said.

Here we go. 'Sure.'

She lowered herself onto the step. 'I moved out of here because my dad's an arse-hole.'

'I gathered that,' said Melvin.

162

She held her look on him.

'Ah, no, what I mean is I know you chose to…'

'It's okay,' she said. 'God, how did Harriet end up with a jumpy little weasel like you?' She smiled at him. 'I'm messing with you. No, everyone one knows my dad is stuck in the Dark Ages. The world is split in two: his world, in his mind, and the real world, out here with the rest of us. Sometimes I wonder if he enjoys being an ignorant, deluded, self-righteous, would-be elitist. But then I think the truth is…he just can't help it. He doesn't know he's a foolish imbecile. But me – I had to go.'

Rose flicked ash onto the step and took another drag.

'Harriet really loves you,' she said. 'It's obvious.'

'I know,' he said.

'Hey, you want some special K?' said Rose.

'What?'

'Special K,' she said. 'Ketamine. It's a tranquilliser. You didn't think I'd sit through this completely straight, did you?'

'Oh, right.' Melvin shook his head. 'I'm okay, thanks.'

Rose flicked her cigarette away and stood up. 'And don't worry about Mum. She comes on to anything with a pair of testicles. Just ignore her and she'll leave you alone.'

Rose disappeared inside the house.

It was almost eleven o'clock. Rose had left to meet some friends, Caroline was clearing up, and Randolph was watching television. Melvin and Harriet sat outside on the doorstep, talking, as they waited for a cab.

'I hope you enjoyed this evening,' she said. 'I know it was a bit crazy.'

He smiled. 'It was cool. They seem nice.'

She kissed him. 'Thanks, darling. I'm popping to the loo, okay?'

She went inside, and Melvin sat staring into the dark street. It *was* a bit crazy. But then, it could have been worse. He couldn't think how, exactly, but he was sure it could have been.

He laughed and shook his head at the thought of Harriet's mum. What a woman.

What would he tell Harriet? Did she know what her mum was like? He took a deep breath and tried to shrug off the pressure.

He heard footsteps behind him, and turned to see Randolph.

'Melvin,' he said.

Randolph was holding a large glass of red wine. He took a step down and sat next to Melvin.

Then he looked straight ahead and said, 'I know my wife fools around, Melvin.'

Melvin said nothing.

'Oh, sure, I'm not stupid,' said Randolph. 'A blind and deaf man could tell you that.' He shook his head and took a sip of wine. 'Yeah, she was always a bit naughty. I knew that when I married her. Silly me, thinking I could tame her. Hmm. No, no, a leopard doesn't change its spots. But you can't blame the leopard.'

Randolph turned to Melvin with a menacing look. 'If I ever find the guy that's messing around with my wife, I'll rip his heart out and feed it to him.'

Melvin was sick with fright. His natural instinct was to run away, away from danger and the possibility of torture.

He swallowed and nodded. Technically, he didn't actually do anything with Caroline.

'I don't know why I'm telling you all this,' said Randolph, looking down. He was calmer now. 'You won't ever have this problem with Harriet. She's a good girl. You can trust her.' He looked at Melvin again. 'Feel free to contribute to this conversation anytime, Melvin.'

'Um, yeah,' said Melvin. 'I really love Harriet. She's definitely the one for me.'

Randolph nodded and actually smiled for once. It was a genuine smile, from a warm place. 'That's what I wanted to hear,' he said. 'There's hope for you yet, boy.'

'Thank you, sir.'

'Cut the crap, Melvin. This isn't the army.'

Melvin heard talking from inside the house. It was Harriet and her mum. What were they discussing?

'I always wanted the best for my kids,' said Randolph. 'Even Simon. He's my boy, you know. My little boy.' Randolph put his face in his hands and began to sob. 'It's not my fault. It's not my fault.'

This was unexpected. Melvin now the shoulder to cry on to Randolph, of all people.

'Hey,' said Melvin, more uncomfortable than ever. 'There is nothing wrong with Simon. Nothing at all.'

'He's a homo.'

Melvin almost laughed, partly from the pain of his own situation, and partly from Randolph's larger than life, slightly misplaced personality.

'I know it might not be what you wanted for Simon,' said Melvin. 'And that's understandable. But Simon's a great guy. He really is. He's successful in his work, he's nice to people, and fun to be around...'

'You sure you don't fancy him?' said Randolph, gaining some composure.

165

'And above all,' said Melvin. 'Simon is really happy. You should be very proud to have a son like him.'

Randolph said nothing. There was the faintest look on his face of something clicking into place.

'And you know what else I think?' said Melvin.

'I've got a feeling you're gonna tell me.'

'I think Simon would be over the moon if he knew his father was behind him.'

Randolph gave him a blank look.

'Ah, that is, behind him in the emotionally supportive sense…'

'I know what you mean,' said Randolph.

There was silence. Melvin could hear his own heartbeat, as Randolph stared into dark space. A car turned the corner, and slowed down, eventually stopping in front of the house.

'Cab for Harriet,' the driver called.

Melvin nodded and stood up.

'It's the missing piece of your puzzle,' he said to Randolph.

Randolph looked down for a moment. 'It's probably too late.'

Melvin shook his head. 'I don't think so.'

Harriet came rushing out. 'Is that the cab?'

She kissed her father goodbye, and she and Melvin walked down to the car hand in hand.

When the car reached the end of the road, Melvin looked back. Randolph was still sitting on the step, alone with his wine.

Poor Lost Poem   MARK ARRAM

A poem of mine's lost
could be anywhere in the school
I pressed print on the computer
but it stayed recorded
as print – to – go
means it might've come out when I had gone
home

Oh poesy
where are you
where are the lines about trees
and morning sunshine I wrote

The next morning
In the best interests of me
I go hunting for it
kinda have to be ruthless
when doing poetry
first stop the office
to see Rosie

Hoovering the Roof

I told her which printer didn't work
she checked the cartridge
full of ink
wiggled all the leads
all connected
sorry
she said
I don't know where it is

I went to the premises manager
the man's broad chested
laid back
used to be a club cricketer
poem
no
I haven't seen one of those around here
where'd you leave it
maybe it got put in the bins
by mistake
why don't you have a look in there

The pm laughed
at the thought of that
and me
rooting in the rubbish
where he once speared dead
a squealing rat

So I went and asked a TA

Poor Lost Poem

one of the Bermondsey girls
whether she'd seen my poem
what's it look like
she asked
eyeing me a bit suspiciously
I shrugged
looked towards the kitchen
usual
I said
single piece of paper
some words written on it
she carried on with her scissors and sticky back
plastic
sorry Mark can't help yer
have you tried the caretaker
I nodded
then it's lost then isn't it

We could both smell fried onions
perhaps a little chili
why don't ya see if it's been cooked
she said a little cruelly

The cook came quickly out of her room
she'd been listening to a voicemail
her Nokia
was the only object
on an otherwise empty office table

she went straight to her cooking

Hoovering the Roof

stirring the onions
adding water from a jug
and told me to get out
like I was some nasty bug

she was afraid would jump up
and hop
into her large steel pot

I stepped back
a bit downhearted
I've lost a poem
have you seen it
cook hardly listened
waved me away with her large wooden spoon
no I haven't seen your poem
then muttered to herself
but loud enough for me to hear
and if I did
d'you think I'd really care

My search went on

the makeshift library
was opposite the kitchen
I scanned the shelves
maybe a resourceful child
had slipped my poem
between the pages of a story

Poor Lost Poem

nothing

I had to give up
couldn't very well interrupt a class lesson
peering through the glass door
of year three
the teacher wasn't holding my poem up
as an example of bad writing
or asking
if it was the work of one of the children

Before I went back to my room
to take consolation in the Word Doc
I wandered up to the head's office
under cover of what was needed for breakfast
club

She was at her desk
peering at some internal policy manual
and in my gentlest most respectful voice
I mentioned that we needed a new box of cereal

The head was too engrossed
and said with a hand pointing
write what I have to get on a post it note
my poem wasn't on top of her filing cabinet
just some laminated photos of children
gospel singing

Hoovering the Roof

Poem less
but somehow heartened
I retreated to my room
relieved that no one seemed to have it
but I got a shock

In **my**
room
sitting at **my**
computer
was the new TA from Tower Hamlets
who has recently started invading my space

I won't be long
she said
just preparing for a dyslexia test
she was writing things down
on a single piece of paper
the backside of a printed sheet
I squinted
my heart missed a beat
it was my poem
about the beautiful morning trees
she looked round and grinned
waved my poem in the air
and said
is this yours
sorry
I found it on the desk
and thought it was scrap

Pluck SOPHIE MONKS KAUFMAN

Bridget had to leap into the road when a woman dragging a mini suitcase affected not to see her. Standing dangerously close to oncoming traffic, Bridget eyed the crowd, waiting for a gap so as to dash through to a safe patch of pavement. An opportunity came as a businessman on a mobile stopped to check his watch, causing another man to walk into him. Bridget dashed through to the pavement and once there adopted her usual posture – head down, feet dragging – as she headed towards the pub.

After turning off Upper Street onto Essex Road, Bridget arrived at the indie pub, where the ceilings were high and the lights were low. There was a fancy literary reading on which meant a slightly more bohemian class of men than this pub usually attracted; all skinny ties, curly hair and superb vocabularies. Merely seeing the array of accessible men was enough to make Bridget's heart beat faster.

Hoovering the Roof

It had been a while since Bridget had seen any action and the result was a constant low-level horniness that would spike in the presence of the men she met during her busy social life. The problem was that she had adopted a passive approach to the men and waited, like a Disney princess, to be whisked off her feet and transported to a world where birds talked and brooms swept up of their own accord.

Bridget's best mate, Georgia, was waving at her from by the bar, dressed, as was her usual style, in sleek purple dress that lovingly stroked her Jessica Rabbit curves.

'Hello darling,' said Georgia, giving her a peck on the cheek.

'Hello.' Bridget pecked back.

'How was work?'

'Groundbreaking. I've been asked to do the reporting for a documentary set in Pakistan.'

'That's amazing. How did that happen?'

'One of the cameramen at *Wake Up!* works for a Pakistani charity and he put me forward.'

'Your star's on the rise, my dear. Remember me when you're at the Beeb.'

Before Bridget had time to answer, a fresh-faced young blade in a baby pink shirt came between them.

They both blushed excitedly and neither spoke. The boy smiled at Bridget and her blush intensified.

'Are you here for the reading?' he asked her.

'Yeah,' she bleated.

The name 'Todd' was called from the corner and a middle-aged man was seen beckoning him.

'Gotta go,' said the boy. 'See you later.'

As he disappeared, Georgia raised an eyebrow.

'Oh, god,' moaned Bridget. 'Yeaaah,' she repeated mockingly.

'Don't worry, darling. The night is young. You can build on that 'yeaah.''

'Unless I devolve, and end up gurgling.'

'This has been known to happen.'

The clock behind the bar read quarter to eight and so the two ordered drinks and then walked upstairs to where the evening's entertainment, a literary death match, was taking place.

'That was absolutely brilliant. Thank you, Georgia,' said Bridget, two hours later, when the final reader had finished the show with a rap.

'It was amazing,' said Georgia. 'Rhyming Gorgonzola with Moldova was inspired.'

'My favourite line was...' She tailed off as she saw the pink-shirted boy of earlier standing in the middle of three women.

'Yes...?'

'Sorry, my favourite line was...'

The three women all burst into laughter.

'Dammit,' murmured Bridget.

'You should go over and talk to him.'

'That's just not me,' said Bridget grimly. 'I meekly stand back doing nothing.'

'So, up your game!'

'No, thank you. I'll just stand here and make defeatist remarks.'

At this point, like an agent of providence, the organiser of the evening walked over and asked if they had been introduced to everyone. He was a worldly and witty man in his mid thirties and asked, 'How's it going, ladies?'

He followed Bridget's wistful line of vision said, 'I'll be right back.'

Moments later he had dived in and extracted the pink-shirted one.

'He doesn't fuck about,' said Georgia as they watched the two men approach them, deeply involved in conversation.

'Todd,' the organiser said, 'this is the lovely Bridget. Bridget, Todd.'

They shook hands and then the process was repeated with Georgia, whilst the organiser seamlessly blended back into the crowd.

Georgia discovered a need for the toilet and Bridget found herself taking in Todd from about a foot away. His face shone with health. He had dark hair, cat eyes and rolled-up shirtsleeves.

'Are you admiring my shirt?' asked Todd, following her gaze.

'Hmmmm,' said Bridget, diplomatically.

Todd laughed. 'I'm only wearing it because my boss was here, that's why I had to dash earlier.'

'Who do you work for?'

'Picador.'

'Sweet! How did you get a job like that?'

'Through someone I knew at Uni.'

'Which Uni did you go to?'

He looked sheepish. 'Er, Oxford.'

'Ah, you're one of the elite.'

'Not exactly,' he said, the ruddy face growing slightly pinker.

'Don't worry; I'm just jealous because they wouldn't let me in. I tried to storm the building and everything.'

He looked at her and smiled. The smile took a long time to form and, when complete, was dangerously charming.

'Shall we go and sit down?' he said, touching her on the arm.

The touch sent a jolt of longing throughout Bridget's nervous system. At this point, one of the girls from Todd's previous conversation waved from her new position on the sofa.

'Shall we?' said Todd to Bridget and, with a smile of resignation plastered to her face, Bridget said,

'Yes, we shall.'

The two walked across wooden floors to one of many long low leather sofas and took their seats beside Rival Girl who immediately engaged Todd – but not Bridget – in a conversation.

'Thank you so much for coming,' she said, eyes imploring behind thick black lashes.

Bridget watched the two figures beside her interact – her earnest, he chilled – and tried not to gag. She turned to see Georgia moving across the floor and leapt up to meet her half way.

Georgia eyed the conversation between Rival Girl and Todd and said, 'Who's that?'

'A girl who's been helping the organiser. I can't work out whether they're flirting or networking.'

The two watched for a while.

'It's a hard one to call, 'continued Bridget. 'It could even be a rare case of two nice people having a chat.'

Georgia laughed. 'Good one.'

The organiser approached slightly shakily, Becks in hand.

'How's it going?' he said.

'I'm not sure,' said Bridget glumly, 'He seems to have lost interest.'

'Are you crazy?' bellowed the organiser. 'I was watching the body language before. He's totally into you.'

'He hasn't made any decisive moves.'

'He's probably just shy,' shouted the organiser, as if this was completely self-evident. He leaned in confidentially. 'Y'know I wouldn't be with my current girl if she hadn't forced me to take her number.'

'Really?'

'It's not just girls that are shy.'

Bridget looked dubiously at the organiser, taking in his American teeth, immaculate hair and smooth New York drawl.

'But what if I throw myself at him and he says no?'

The organiser placed a reassuring hand on Bridget's shoulder. 'You've got to make out with a lot of dolts to meet a prince and you've got to flirt with a lot of dolts to get them to make out with you. Romance is a numbers game, babe.'

He took a swig of Becks whilst Georgia and Bridget looked at him adoringly, like he was Barack Obama. Georgia said, 'Do you have any like-minded friends who are single?'

'Right over there, babe. Let me introduce you to them. Are you cool now, Bridge?'

Bridget looked to the seating area where Rival Girl was putting on her coat and Todd was not.

'I'm cool,' said Bridget.

They walked together down Pentonville Road towards Kings Cross, talking about the book launch he was attending for three big American writers next week. They talked about literature. They had similar tastes and the smiles and dry remarks just kept coming. When they got to Kings Cross, the big station clock beamed out one o'clock and they waited together at the same bus stop. Six teenagers were play fighting in the road and a man with a pockmarked face lurked in the shadows. A bus came that went to Notting Hill. Even though she lived in Brixton, Bridget climbed aboard with him.

The bus terminated at Notting Hill Gate and he turned to her.

'Right, I'm going that way, what's the next leg of your journey?'

It took Bridget a while to compute. She blinked.

'Ah, I guess I'll get a cab?'

It was a question.

'Good idea, I'll help you hail one. Actually, forget that, I'm really tired, do you mind if I go home?'

'It's fine,' said Bridget.

He turned to kiss her on the cheek and, feeling her last chance slipping away, she turned her face so that her mouth was on his. He froze and then withdrew.

'Lovely to meet you,' he cried, backing away. 'I'll see you at the next one of these.'

Bridget raised a limp hand and watched him recede.

It was Wednesday rush hour and Bridget glided out of Angel station, smoothly side-stepping the wave of commuters who were not looking where they were going. Once she found a clear stretch of pavement, she padded rapidly towards the park bench where Georgia was waiting for her. When their eyes met, Georgia began laughing.

'Hellooooo, Casanova,' she yelled.

'I can't believe I followed him home,' moaned Bridget, but she was smiling.

'You didn't follow him *home*.... just to his neighbourhood.'

'I thought he liked me.'

'He might have done.'

'I think we can be sure that he didn't.'

'Well, the important thing is you gave it your best shot.'

'I certainly did that.'

'And that took pluck.'

'True.'

'And pluck is much sexier than cowardice.'

'Also true.'

'Now, you just need to maybe refine your modus operandi. It's not practical to follow all your crushes home.'

Laughing, the girls got to their feet and headed off towards the theatre.

Domestic HELEN HARDY

Shards of a broken vase

curl like petals in your garden of turbulence.

I gather them up,

soft as the shadows under my eyes,

knowing I will be gone by morning.

Debi Alper has been a member of EDWG since the early days. As a direct result, she has completed five novels in the Nirvana series of thrillers set in SE London. The first two, *Nirvana Bites* and *Trading Tatiana*, have been published by Weidenfeld & Nicolson. She is currently working on a sixth stand alone novel. These days, Debi writes full time and avoids the traditional lifestyle of authors not on the best-sellers' list (boiling old shoes to make soup to feed their families) by working as a freelance editor and mentor. She also hosts creative writing workshops.

Debi's website is www.debialper.co.uk

She blogs at http://debialper.blogspot.com

Mark Arram started the East Dulwich Writers' Group armed with a seedy pack of white postcards, with the intention of getting out of his seedier bedsit and into the rather more comfortable homes of literary Dulwich women. There was also something to do with wanting to meet strangers with similar literary tastes to his own, to listen to and appreciate his poetry.

Joanna Czechowska is a journalist and has written short stories for magazines such as *Best, The Lady, That's Life* and *Woman*. She joined EDWG in 2007. Her debut novel, *The Black Madonna of Derby*, draws on her early experiences of life with a Polish father and growing up in the immigrant Polish community in Derby. The novel was also published in Polish in Poland under the title *Goodbye Polsko* and became a bestseller. *The Black Madonna of Derby* is published by Silkmill Press at £7.99.

Rachael Dunlop spent many years wanting to be a writer but didn't know how to start. And there was always something else that needed doing more urgently – like cleaning out the fluff from behind the toilet. When she finally ran out of excuses, she took a creative writing course and hasn't stopped writing since. Rachael writes short stories in various genres, a selection of which can be found at her website, along with her blog and photography. Rachael was the winner of the NYC Midnight Creative Writing Championships 2009. She would quite like to write a novel now, if only she knew how to start.
http://web.me.com/rachaeldunlop1/Butterflies/Welcome.html,

Amy Griggs edits an education magazine and writes short stories for both adults and children. She joined EDWG because she hoped meetings would scare her into finishing a novel. When she isn't writing, Amy likes Guinness, cricket and cheesecake – although not necessarily at the same time. Her short story, *New York Boots*, was inspired by a real and much loved pair of knee-highs. After immigrating to England, the boots were kidnapped by an irate ex-boyfriend and imprisoned in a dark cupboard. Three months passed before they managed to escape to Crystal Palace, where they now share a flat with some cricket boots and a pair of red patent shoes.

Helen Hardy loves the challenge of condensing ideas and feelings into poetry and short stories. With the invaluable support of EDWG, she is also venturing into longer fiction and has almost completed her first novel *Mother of the World*, set in Cairo during the Second World War. Helen lives in Norwood and is now researching a future novel inspired by the area's history.

Kathleen Hinwood. Amongst the possessions stolen by a removal company were the two novels that Kathleen wrote. Leaving no trace, she has begun again, writing in fits and starts, with a particular focus on short stories. A fairly new member to EDWG, Australian by birth, Kathleen lives in Hither Green.

Sue Jennings has been writing for three years. She joined EDWG in the spring of 2009. Sue taught Secondary English and A-Level Psychology for ten years, before taking a break in 2005 to rest and write. She writes short stories and poems and is working (slowly) on a novel. Her stories are mostly based on her experiences of various people and their relationships in a small seaside town while she was living part-time on an old boat near the Sussex coast. Sue has one daughter and three grand-daughters, who she sees every week. She has two dogs, and enjoys cycling and spending time near the water. She keeps a boat in London's docklands. Sue moved to London in 2006, and helps to run a day nursery with her partner, who is an artist. Her poetry emerged as a result of having more limited time for writing, and is based on the observations and emotions of a changed lifestyle. She has recently begun entering short story and poetry competitions. As yet, none of her work has been published.

Mark Kiely grew up in South London, has travelled quite a bit, and now works as an acupuncturist in East Dulwich. Following the horrors of the July 7th bombings in 2005, his short story, *A New Beginning*, is intended as a celebration of public transport in London. Every single day, this is an environment where the passion of human existence takes place. Those who fail to see this, fail to see the wonder of creation.

Becca Leathlean worked in journalism for fifteen years before changing careers and doing a Master's degree in Criminology. She then got a job setting up restorative justice projects, enabling offenders to make amends to the victims of their crimes. A 'restorative parks' project in Reading was the inspiration behind a community garden (the Stanstead Strip in Forest Hill) that she started with neighbours on moving back to London. A career change later, Becca has just opened a shop in Sydenham selling Spanish goods, local crafts and olive oil, and hopes to satisfy a secret desire to run an arts-café by opening a tea room and art gallery at the back. Becca joined EDWG early in 2009 and is enjoying writing fiction with the encouragement and very constructive criticism of the group.

Emma MacKinnon
Goes to school.
Comes home. Cooks tea.
Writes and paints.
Gets on with stuff.
Doesn't get on with stuff.
Likes a bit of rock 'n' roll.
(Has been close to going to work in slippers – but so far common sense has prevailed.)

Daniel Maitland, poet and songwriter, released his debut solo album last year, ***Rumours Of A Nice Day***, on Folkwit records. He is a regular on the London music and spoken word scene. He has written two novels, one for children and one for adults, plus a miserable-ist's travelogue – called ***The Black Diary***. None of which are yet published – other than a few Lulu versions for friends. His poetry has been featured on Sky TV and in a few UK magazines such as *The New Writer*, and was shortlisted in a number of national poetry competitions, including Faber and Faber. His words have been set by the North Sea Radio Orchestra and a number of other artists, including: Melanie Blatt, Nick Homes and members of the Stereo MC's. He has a bumper poetry collection, ***Even Bad Dogs do Good Things*** on sale now at a few good bookshops and at gigs. Daniel played for ten years with soul legend Geno Washington, and worked in a number of other writing and performing projects – including the RSC and The Foundations. He currently works part time for the New Deal scheme, mentoring unemployed musicians, writers and other admirable layabouts, and collects 'We really quite liked it but due the current climate...' rejection letters from agents.
www.myspace.com/danielmaitland

Ferdi Mehmet enjoys stories and books of various genres. At the time of writing his short story, ***Dinner with the
Colemans***, he was fascinated with character-driven narrative,
and dialogue – a factor unlikely to change. 'In life it is people
and their relationships that are intriguing, so that kind of fiction appeals to me.' Ferdi completed his first novel, ***Broken***, a
multi-story drama, in 2008. He is working on another novel,
and writes screenplays, short stories, and poetry. He joined
EDWG in 2009 and loves the support, feedback, and encouragement from the group.

'Although fiction is technically the untrue, a lie...to me
good fiction is often about using the imagination to tell the
truth – the truth in that web of illusion.'

Marti Mirkin likes to understand things and she likes
to reach a place of moderation in herself.... would say so far
there's only modest success on both these paths.... She loves
her children, her friends, her dog, the outdoors, words, music,
holding and being held, sitting quietly, eating, swimming in
the ocean, conversation and laughing, bright colours and subtle colours.... She knows too much about being sad and would
like to know what to do next... She likes taking risks, growing
and changing, but doesn't know why it takes so long... if
we passed in the street she'd smile and say hello first, being
not at all shy.

Sophie Monks Kaufman is a well-meaning simpleton who is still trying to find the right words. The few grains of intellect she has that aren't directed towards rabid socialising are spent editing the *Culture Vulture* section for *The London Word*. *The London Word* is – without a shred of bias – probably one of the best blogs in the world, ever. Other projects include an autobiographical novel about a year spent in an adolescent unit at the tender age of sixteen. Sophie recommends a year in a unit to all slightly repressed, middle-class girls seeking an outlet for madness – although it does have a side effect of upsetting your parents and is best left off the CV. Sophie loves everyone who can tell it like it is without losing their sense of humour. Humour is everything.

Anand Nair writes about Indian women because she sees how they struggle between respecting tradition and following their own stars. In the ensuing fray, they get diminished and a little tattered, like herself. However, more and more of them are now literate/educated, earning a living. In the end, there is nothing to beat education (and economic independence) in knocking down fences in the mind. She should know – having spent a lifetime in education in Africa and England. Her first novel, *A Streak of Sandalwood*, due out before Christmas, pursues this theme at greater length.

Kate Rose graduated with a First Class degree from King's College, London, in 1994. After setting up a health clinic in Mayfair, she published a non-fiction book on heart disease and stroke prevention; wrote for various publications on health, food and travel; designed a brand of juice drinks and appeared on LBC radio. Having completed an MA in Creative and Life Writing at Goldsmith's University, and inspired by her South London surroundings, she wrote *The Hidden Phases of Venus*, an historical novel spanning the 1860s to present day; exploring the quest of two women as they attempt to reconcile freedom, love and art. Kate lives with her husband and sixteen month old daughter in a house close to Dulwich Woods where you will find, in a small dell, the ruins of an old folly.

Richard Woodhouse's first novel, *Deathless*, is a ghostly tale of detectives, death, and deception set in Herne Hill and Brixton (sorry Dulwich) and is recommended reading for those who like their crime on the spooky side. Still in search of an agent/publisher, *Deathless* remains available only from lulu.com. Richard is in the process of writing his second novel, *Mr. Reed* – a gothic tale of love and transformation. *Les Tournesols*, the short story in this anthology, was inspired by the heat and haze of a holiday in France. If anyone knows the answer as to why sunflowers face east when they stop turning, please let him know.

For all things Richard Woodhouse go to www.rhkw.co.uk

EAST DULWICH WRITERS' GROUP

Hoovering the Roof

earwig press
edwg.co.uk

Lightning Source UK Ltd.
Milton Keynes UK
11 March 2010

151229UK00002B/5/P